FRENCH MEMSAHIB

TAYA
ZINKIN

Thomas Harmsworth Publishing
Stoke Abbott

First Published 1989

British Library Cataloguing in Publication Data
Zinkin, Taya
French memsahib.
1. India, 1936-1947. Biographies
I. Title
954.03'59'0924
ISBN 0-948807-08-3

Typset by A.D.L

Printed and bound in Great Britain by
Biddles Ltd, Guildford and King's Lynn

To Maurice's ICS
and
to our beloved grand-daughter
Kate

INDIA IN 1947

1

I thought India was French

Geography was never my best subject. I thought India was French. Dakar, Ouagadougou, Pondichéry, Chandernagore, Yanaon, Karikal, Mahé . . . all French. As French as Saigon or Tananarive.

At school, there was an Indian girl a few years older; I used to stare at her a lot. She wore a tiny diamond studded in her nostril. It matched diamond earrings . . . unheard of for a little girl. We never spoke. She was at least three years ahead of me. I admired her suntan and envied her hair. She was petite, small boned. She slithered as she walked, her shiny plait dangling behind her, silken and incredibly black. In my form she was known as 'l'Indienne'. Was the diamond screwed into her nose? Did it stay there at night? Did it hurt when she blew? I used to speculate each time I saw her. Later, when I lived in India I could have asked, but somehow never did. To this day I don't know.

By the time I was ten I knew the Jungle Book by heart. In French of course. Our governess used to take turns with me to read it out loud to my little brother. Not once, not twice, not thrice, many times. For a whole year we spent a couple of hours with Mowgli before going to bed. Akela's death never failed to draw tears. It never occurred to me that Kipling was not French like Jules Verne and Hector Malo. Looking back, this was odd since I had begun to learn English at school, pitting myself against Dickensian prose. To our governess I owe the 'Just So Stories', Kipling's tales and 'Kim' - as perfect in translation as in the original. Dupleix's exploits as extolled by the history teacher left a vague feeling that if North India - Kim's India - was partly English, the India that really mattered was French. The truth is that I gave India no thought until I saw a film with Tyrone Power cast as a handsome Indian doctor struggling to contain a cholera epidemic. My interest had been doubly aroused: as a fan of Tyrone Power and as a medical student. I was sufficiently stirred to read the book on which the film is based and I briefly indulged in fantasy. Like the heroine, I played my part in helping to save Indians.

My next encounter with India was strangely disturbing. I was taken to see Ram Gopal and his troupe of dancers at the theatre. A devotee of the Ballets Russes I had never seen anything like it. The experience was more physical than artistic. Bent-kneed, open-thighed, thrusting to the beat of anklets and drums, the dancers were embodying desire with such vigour that I found myself throbbing in my seat.

Such was my ignorance of matters Indian that the first time I came across Gandhi's name was at a fancy dress ball. An exceedingly hairy youth, draped in a sheet with a kitchen alarm-clock dangling from his neck, announced himself as 'Mahatma Gandhi'.

'Who is Mahatma Gandhi?' I asked.

'Haven't you heard of India's naked Fakir?' For a time, from then on, Gandhi's name evoked rope tricks, nail-beds and snake charmers. I was not a newspaper reader. Medical School absorbed me leaving just enough time for friendships and heartbreaks, none for current events beyond the antics of Hitler and the imminence of war.

The first Indian I got to know was Dr Sharma. By the time our paths crossed the war was in full swing. After a long and chequered journey enlivened by varied adventures I had landed a Research Assistantship in an American University. Dr Sharma and I shared a laboratory. He was a friendly, podgy little man with heavily oiled black hair and short fingers which he used to flex back whenever he got involved in deep thought. He could bend his thumbs back against his wrists. Quiet, self-contained, we might never have got beyond a casual word or two had it not been for the pigeon-holes which served as letter boxes.

'So you know someone in India?' Dr Sharma greeted me when one of my letters, its cover badly torn, had been mistakenly put in his pigeon-hole by the porter unable to decipher what was left of my name.

'Yes, a chap I met in England years ago.'

'Oh, Oh! In the Army is he?'

'No, in Government.'

Dr Sharma eyed me curiously, his eyes even blacker and shinier with excitement. 'In the ICS could it be?'

'Yes. In the ICS.'

'And what does he do?'

'I don't know.' This was quite true. Maurice Zinkin never mentioned work in his letters. I only knew that he was the paying-guest of a Joint Secretary to the Government of India whose wife took a leading part in amateur theatricals and that he shared Jane, a horse of British ancestry, with a Viceregal ADC. I told Dr Sharma all I knew. Sucking air through his teeth, flexing his fingers back until it hurt to watch, he decreed:

'Then he must be high up and doing important work.'

From then on Dr Sharma's attitude to me underwent a subtle change. If he saw me carrying anything heavy he would insist on taking over. When he had to make a trip to the store-room a couple of flights below our lab he never failed to enquire whether I needed something.

'Really it is no bother, no bother at all. Just tell me and I will bring it. No need two of us going down.' He even went so far as to offer to clean my equipment and keep an eye over slow, time-consuming reactions, 'You go and have lunch. No need for you to stay. Fear not. I am here anyway.

Ess, do go please.' Dr Sharma pronounced 'yes' as 'ess', but for 'eggs' he always said 'yeggs'.

I found his solicitude so cloying that I would have put a drastic end to it had Maurice's letters not become more frequent and more intimate. I wanted to find out as much as possible as I could about India.

Dr Sharma was married and had two children. His marriage had, like all Indian marriages, been arranged by his parents.

'They took my horoscope to the marriage broker and asked for it to be matched with that of an Iengar girl.' Iengars, he explained, were the top caste of South Indian Brahmins. For an Iengar to marry, say, an Iyer, the next caste down of South Indian Brahmins, was as much out of the question as . . . searching for an example he tortured his thumbs . . . 'It is like in America a white marrying a negro.'

Dr Sharma saw Apurna for the first time during the wedding ceremony. 'I am lucky. She is tall and very fair skinned. She is an excellent cook and she can play the veena. I will bring to show you the picture she sent me. She is very thoughtful my Apurna. I am not old-fashioned like my parents, I welcome a daughter especially since we already have a son.' On a stool beside the ubiquitous potted palm and painted screen of photographic studios sat a handsome woman draped in a sari covering her head. On her forehead an ornamental piece of jewelry stopped short of a dot painted between her eyes. It hung above the root of her nose which was studded with an ornament four times bigger than that of the girl in my school. Apurna's nose-piece matched the brooch which held her sari firmly in place on one shoulder . . . A baby on her lap stared at the camera, its dark eyes strangely enlarged with soot. A spot of soot marred her otherwise pretty little face. A small boy stood by his mother's side, dressed in a brocade frock coat. I could not help asking what was wrong with the baby's eyes.

'Nothing is wrong. We use khol around the eyes. It keeps

flies away, cuts down the glare and acts as disinfectant. And the spot on Lakshmi's cheek. That is to keep away the evil eye. If parents boast that their baby is beautiful and perfect it angers the Gods. So it is our custom, when children are very young, to give them a blemish.' Dr Sharma went on to say that since infant mortality in India is very high one could not be too careful.

Having Dr Sharma to dinner used to be quite a to-do. A strict vegetarian, he did not eat processed cheese because it had been made with rennet. Fruit, salads, nuts, cottage-cheese, yoghurt, bread he could eat but he would not touch pasta in case it contained 'yeggs'.

He drew up for me a reading list on India. The 'Rigveda' which I took out of the library made so little sense that I did not persevere beyond the first few pages. Forster's 'Passage to India' I found very depressing.

After I read Gandhi's compelling autobiography I decided to stop reading about India. I had by then become engaged to Maurice and instinct told me to wait until I could find out at first hand.

The news of my engagement was received by some with mixed feelings. Dr Sharma bought me a travelling sewing-kit.

'A small present to remind you that there was a time when we were friends.' He suddenly added with bitterness: 'Now you are going to be a Burra Memsahib and join the Heaven-Born, you will cease to know me. If I ever come to Delhi you will receive me on the verandah, but you will not invite me inside.'

Dr Baumgarten, my Director of Studies, asked me into his office.

'I hear you are planning to marry an Englishman. I feel it my duty to warn you to think twice before you take the plunge. I spent a year doing post-graduate research at King's College Cambridge. When I got back to America I wept with joy. The English are such awful snobs. This man in India, how do you know he is not a homosexual? So many Englishmen are. You don't know what you are letting yourself in for.'

Dr Baumgarten was quite right. I did not know Maurice . . . and yet . . . one cannot correspond with someone for nine years without getting some idea.

2

The Heaven-Born

We had met, in 1936, fleetingly. I was in London on holiday, ostensibly to improve my English, in reality to get over an unrequited infatuation. My stay was drawing to its close when I was invited to visit a girls' college in Cambridge. From Girton I was taken to a sherry party given by the brother of one of the girls. I did not stay long; half an hour at the most. Long enough for a handsome six-footer to flirt with me and suggest I be walked to the station. Waving goodbye from the carriage window, I suddenly realized that I had left behind, wrapped in a newspaper, the ash-tray I had stolen from the restaurant car of the London and North Eastern Railway. Metallic, fairly large, it was embossed with the company's initials - a prize addition to my collection. Collecting stolen ash-trays used to be a craze. At the outbreak of war I had 850. Scribbling my address on a scrap of paper I tossed it out of the window and asked that my parcel be sent on to Paris. It duly arrived, accompanied by a few friendly words. A thank-you letter was called for.

Thus began the correspondence I might not have kept up had he not been so handsome and had his letters not ended with 'Love, Maurice'. I remember blushing. 'Love!' So soon. We had been less than an hour together, and never alone. Miss Caruel, my English teacher, had taught us to finish letters with 'Yours Sincerely'. We corresponded. Maurice's letters were pompous, earnest, stilted and difficult to decipher. Had

I known that the French equivalent for 'love' at the end of a letter is 'amicalement' I would have stopped. Blessed be my ignorance and my vanity.

After he went to India his letters, which sometimes took a couple of months to arrive, were mildly interesting at first. But very soon they, too, became boring. Maurice must have sensed this.

'It is difficult to be amusing. I think overwork knocks it out of me. But you may like the story of the village headman who, when asked what three times twelve was, answered, after deep thought and much calculation, 'twenty four'. I am sorry you find I am getting 'fonctionnaire', but alone in the District, with everybody wanting some benefit from you, it is rather difficult to keep your sense of proportion. I suppose the Supernumerary Assistant Collector is not terribly important because the place where he is important is itself so remote and minor, but although it is a very small pond, in that pond he really is a very big fish and so it is easy to forget and get self-important.

'This is rather a long apology, but I would not like you to think that I am falling already into the ICS defect of considering myself God, or as they say here, Heaven-Born.'

Our correspondence, interrupted by the Fall of France and the Exodus, might never have been resumed had it not been for my father.

After an eventful and prolonged flight from German Occupation we landed in the West Indies where we spent over a year waiting for an American visa. I was continuing my medical studies and having a good time but father was bored. He found enforced idleness intolerable. To kill time he threw himself into the systematic cataloguing of his bulky stamp collection. On reaching 'India' he had a brainwave.

'Why don't you write to that bloke from India? Ask him to send me used stamps. You know, the kind in packets; they are quite cheap. If necessary, I will pay for them.'

'I haven't heard from him in over two years. The last

time he was in some remote panther infested jungle protecting tribals from moneylenders. I have lost his address'.

'Doesn't matter, write just the same. Who knows? If you put India on the envelope it might get there. It's worth a try.' Once Father got an idea into his head . . . 'Have you written to that bloke from India?' he kept asking . . . For peace's sake I did. Amazingly the letter addressed 'Maurice Zinkin Esq, ICS India' reached its destination.

'Thank you for your letter which was a welcome relief after so long a time. I had been wondering what had happened to you.

'You must have had a perfectly frightful time. In fact, you make me ashamed when I think of what you have been through. Even now, here in India, the war has hardly touched us. Work is a little bit harder, things which have to be imported are rather more expensive, we all try to give or lend what we can to the government. And that is all. In my Service we are not allowed to join up, not allowed to do anything except stick to a job which is hardly changed in essentials from peacetime.

'Of course in England it is different but judging from the letters I have from home, it looks as if people were carrying on and accepting things pretty much as they come. So it really does look as if there's reason for every hope about the outcome of the war, though it has perhaps been fortunate the British are a slow-minded people and don't recognize defeat when they see it, as the Germans complain. Even in July, when things were at their worst, and it really did look as if we might lose, my mother, though she was reduced to her last resource, her trust in God, never faltered in her belief we would win. I just don't think it occurred to her or to most English people, that we could lose the war. And I think perhaps she is right, though after the disasters that have come through the negligence induced by over-optimism, one feels as if it will be dangerous ever to be optimistic again.' (February 1942).

Maurice was now living in Bombay, in great style, as his address 'Bombay Castle' suggested. As an Under-Secretary in Residence he had the top of the Bombay Secretariat to himself.

'I have asked two colleagues to live with me. I am not sure you would approve of the company they keep when they are off duty. They are bachelors and they keep trying to fix me up with some girl. I appreciate their intention but would rather keep myself for the woman I shall marry.

'The truth is that we are horribly sex-starved. With the huge number of troops now in India, and the ban on the entry of European women that has been going on for three years, there are about a hundred men for every unmarried girl and a very high proportion of those unmarried girls are either spoilt or dumb. You have to work for a woman here, and after a long day in the office you don't have an awful lot of chance in open competition with the Cavalry on leave. So we just sublimate and hope that when we do one day get leave, we won't be too dazzled by going back to a society in which there are more women than men. Heavenly thought!

'It is no good recommending Hindu mistresses to me. Firstly, it is not done in my service and the good name of the Service means quite a lot to me. Secondly, the properly brought up Hindu girl does not play around, and I am a snob about whom I go to bed with. I have never yet been able to dissociate a woman's body from her mind and manners. It is so very sordid to sleep with somebody one can neither talk to the following morning nor introduce to one's friends the next evening. Sordid for oneself, humiliating for her. India is a place where society is still fairly small and, even in Bombay, the ICS is still conspicuous. It is not possible to go anywhere without the risk of being seen and people are pretty quick to sum up the class of one's companion'.

In sharp contrast to his former letters there was no mention of work. In response to a letter asking what he was doing I got the following answer:

'I feel I must have told you before. The ICS is the Indian Civil Service, the Service to which I have the honour to belong. The Service is restricted to roughly a thousand, half English, half Indian. Most of the top jobs of India's administration are reserved for us. At the moment, of course, we are appallingly short. The war has stopped recruitment so that we are about 10% under strength, and there are about twice as many jobs to do as before. So we have had to promote Provincial Service people and bring in outsiders on a large scale, not always with happy results. There is a perpetual argument between the Centre and the Provinces, and between Departments, over who is to have which ICS officer. It tends to mean that we get the hardest jobs or the ones in which the biggest mess has been made and then get moved on to the next mess.

'That is of course the ICS view of ourselves. Others might tell you that we are rigid bureaucrats without imagination or sympathy, bent only on exploitation and holding up all development by our red-tape. You will have to decide what is the truth for yourself'.

His India was so remote from the world in which I was fighting to survive that I did not even bother to mention our tribulations, not even our stint in a Cuban jail. Instead I wrote about Haiti and the Dominican Republic, the flowers, the fruit, and in due course about my getting engaged to a budding diplomat. Maurice, too, had got engaged to a Bombay beauty, 'I wish you could meet her. She is sweet-tempered, a thoroughly nice girl, very pretty, with flaming red hair'.

The letters announcing our disengagements crossed.

By the time we landed in America Maurice had been transferred to the Finance and Commerce Pool, whatever that meant, and lived in New Delhi. His letters, entirely filled with gossip, would have remained unanswered had they not ended in the same misleading way at a time when I was homesick for France and bitterly resented the quota for women in American medical schools which was forcing me to wait for another five years before I could finish medicine when I only had one more year to study.

I could have joined the Fighting French as a doctor but, with my brother in the American Army, I felt it my duty to stay with my parents who did not know English. I got a Research Fellowship in Biochemistry with the prospect that, at the end of three years, I would get a PhD as well as an MD. It was the hope of getting into medical school through the back door which kept me going for I did not find work with rats exciting.

Maurice claims I proposed. This is partly true. All my friends were either in France or prisoners of war in Germany. His letters were the only link with my past. I had been working with rats for two boring years when I received the following letter:

'Imagine my embarrassment when, having accepted their invitation to spend my week's leave, I realised they expected me to fall for their niece. A nice girl on the rebound from a broken engagement. I like Rosemary a lot but she is not my cup of tea - too flat-chested. I am not her cup of tea either. Things got a bit awkward with broad hints like 'Why don't the two of you go and watch dusk at Sunset Point?' or 'Why don't you take a rickshaw to The Mall and go to Wenger's for tea?' I pleaded work as an excuse to cut my stay in Simla short. Rosemary is an extremely nice girl; I have no doubt that she will soon find someone. Simla is full of glamorous officers on convalescence or on leave from the front, with plenty of time on their hands - and there are so few eligible girls.'

After that letter the tone of my letters changed. Hitherto, like Maurice's, they had been impersonal, the kind exchanged by pen-friends of the same sex.

As my letters became more personal his became more frequent. More intimate. Soon I had to send my photograph. The one he sent me was an amateur snapshot showing a horse under a mango tree. The dense foliage obscured the rider's head. The text more than made up for the disappointing picture. It was bursting with passion.

'I fell in love with you at first sight, that day in Cambridge. I can still see you in that pull-over which set your figure off so well. For years you have been haunting my dreams . . . 'Only fear of rejection had prevented him from declaring himself . . . It went on for page after page with a lack of restraint which made me blush at the thought that feelings so private had been read by a censor. Then came a telegram.

'FORGOT ASK STOP WILL YOU MARRY ME STOP MAURICE'

Instead of wiring 'YES' I wrote to accept.

This was unintentionally inconsiderate. Airmail between America and India took anything up to a month.

Ten thousand miles and nine years separated us but now that the die had been cast we could not wait. Our main problem was getting together. We tried to get married by proxy. This proved impossible under British law. Our only chance was to get married in England. Maurice began to move mountains. I received a formal proposal of marriage witnessed by: The Hon Sir Jeremy Raisman, Finance Member Government of India; The Hon Sir Akbar Hydari, Member for Commerce and Industry; Sir George Abell, Private Secretary to the Viceroy; and by Lieutenant General Sir Francis Tuker of North Africa fame.

Armed with that formidable document I went to the British Consul in New York and was issued with an 'A-One' priority for the next convoy to Europe. In the meantime Maurice, who had been granted compassionate leave, had flown to England in the bomber bringing the Duke of Gloucester back from inspecting South Eastern Command. His flight took four days. My convoy took twenty-one days between New York and Liverpool.

3

Marriage at first sight

Sitting in the hotel lounge I was so nervous that I kept jumping up at every newcomer. Maurice would be arriving soon. What was he like? The photographs I had sent him were flattering. Would he be disappointed? The crossing had been dreadful. The troop-ship was overcrowded. Shortly after leaving New-York a great storm played havoc. There had been casualties from collapsing bunks; most of the crockery had been smashed; the showers had become unusable and there was widespread food poisoning on board. Towards the end of the journey we had been chased by U-boats. Ours had been the last German submarine activity of the war. Torpedoes aimed at the ship I was in, the largest in the convoy, hit two aviation-fuel carriers which exploded, and also two smaller troop-ships which sank at once in the rough sea. There were no survivors. As long as the chase lasted we had to camp on the top deck, strapped in life-jackets, sleeping on the floor.

On entering Liverpool's protected waters I rang Maurice to let him know I had arrived. After more than two weeks without as much as a shower, I was dying for a bath and a change. Instead of the two single rooms I had booked in my name at the Adelphi Hotel they had given me one double room.

'No matter, when Mr. Zinkin arrives, send him up'. The receptionist, an elderly spinster, winced as I explained: 'It's all right. We are getting married.

'Most certainly not! This is a respectable hotel'. She crossed my name off the register. Except for the powder-room there had been nowhere to tidy up. I retreated to a corner of the lounge and ordered a double whisky. My stockings were laddered, my crumpled skirt was stained with lubricating oil, I had lost half the buttons of my jacket, my blouse was peppered with soot. To take my mind off the mess I was in, I tried to imagine what Maurice would look like. After sending me that snapshot on horseback he had written: 'Dearest, the other day I took advantage of a trip to Bombay to get myself properly photographed by Van Dyck and Rembrandt. They are the best photographers in India. As it is rather large I am sending you my portrait under separate cover. I hope you will like it'. It got lost in the post.

An elderly gentleman who had been observing me came over. 'You are obviously waiting for someone. Do you mind if I keep you company? I have to wait a couple of hours for my train'. I could have kissed him. It did not take long before I told him everything. The stolen ash-tray, the nine years, the ordeal of our convoy, the sinking of the ships . . .

'What a story! My dear child, what a romance! We must drink to your happy future. I insist.' He ordered half a bottle of champagne. By the time he left I was relaxed.

An unexpected 'Darling!' jerked me awake. Was I drunk? The man calling me 'Darling' did not look even remotely like I remembered.

Panic nailed me speechless to my seat. Maurice Zinkin looked a sight. Half a dozen cuts and grazes testified to the excitement with which he must have shaved. His thick mop of hair had recently been cut, badly. Barely three inches taller than myself, he wore a suit a couple of sizes too big, a faded greeny-grey suit with pinkish pin-stripes which bore an uncanny resemblance to the zoot-suits favoured in America by the negro poor. 'Thank God that kind old man has left!' flashed through my mind. I had been bragging to him so. Had the crossing not been so horrendous I would have fled back to America. I forced myself to look into Maurice's eyes. Beautiful, moving eyes. I must hold my tongue . . . not say anything rash . . . give ourselves a chance . . . in all those letters, beside the passion there had been such generosity, such striking integrity. In all the years, he had not shot a single tiger, just one little panther. Anyone less honest would have claimed a bull's eye or two . . . especially in those letters, before the war, when he was out in the jungle with Purviz and Zarine, a couple well-known for their skill against tigers . . . In my panic it was his repeated descriptions of missing which tilted the balance . . . I would give him three days before making up my mind.

We were married by special licence, on the first of May 1945. As it had been snowing during the night I had a white wedding.

Maurice's best friend from the ICS, home on sick-leave, was our best man. He came from Northern Scotland the day before the wedding and stayed with us. Two years Maurice's senior, his affection for one he dubbed a 'cream-puff', like all Englishmen, was tinted with motherly concern. Slim, wiry, stubborn, he was delightfully eccentric. A classical scholar, he was wont to lay down the law and savoured audiences.

I took to him at once but put my foot in it announcing that, after Maurice, he was the nicest Englishman I had met so far.

'I am not, I repeat not, English!' he thundered, waving a half-full tumbler with such vigour that centrifugal force, overcoming gravity, his whisky flew to the floor. 'Never, you understand, but never insult a Scot by calling him English!' I was beginning to mumble something when he added, 'but of course, being a foreigner, you can be forgiven'. Smiling with both eyes he declared: 'Maurice is lucky. You will do'. We were sitting in the kitchen, alone together for the first time. 'You don't know how we all worried when that cream-puff of yours got himself engaged. Most unsuitable she was, from every point of view. Very pretty but domiciled.'

'What is domiciled?'

He explained that she had been born and brought up in India. Anglo-Indian mother, father police superintendent, not in the Imperial Service. The wrong background.

'Maurice is such a gentleman. To point this out would have been fatal. It would have become a point of honour with him to see it through. There was only one thing to do and play the game so that it was she, not he, who broke it off. We worked out a plan'. Both the Indian and British members of the Service welcomed her with open arms, but in a manner calculated to make her feel out of place. She had never heard of Bach. She had the oddest standards.

'I remember her saying, quite seriously, that Premy was no lady. Premy - wait till you meet her, she is the prettiest Indian ICS wife - an absolute pet. To say that Premy, who was educated at St. Paul's, is no lady because she doesn't curl her little finger when she holds a teacup - can you imagine! And even if the lass had not been domiciled, she would have been quite wrong for Maurice. They had nothing, not a single thing, in common. She wanted to go out, dance, have a good time. Your cream-puff is not that type. Once, when he took her to a dance at the Royal Bombay Yacht Club, she asked him to get her a corsage. He gave her the money and told her to get it herself. He had not the slightest idea of how to court a woman. He is a blue-stocking, a book-worm, a very fine brain in an egg-head. But then he was not top of his year in the ICS with a hundred marks more than the next man for nothing. Treble Starred Firsts don't grow on trees. But when it comes to day-to-day matters he is a babe in the woods. A heart of gold, but strictly limited interests. She would have got bored with him in no time and taken lovers'.

Inspired by another generous helping of whisky, Robin went on. 'The ICS is a very select club. It is not for nothing that it is called the Iron Frame. It literally holds India together with a handful of chosen men. Some of us pretend otherwise, but it is work that makes us tick. Our sense of duty, our esprit de corps. Work must take precedence. ICS wives need stamina and guts. Those without take to drink or lovers. The trouble is that the English don't believe in educating girls. Unlike we Scots or the Irish. It's a great mistake. The English Memsahibs are costing us the Empire. To be successfully married to a Heaven-Born, as they sometimes call us, a woman has to have inner resources'.

With a sudden blush Robin apologised. 'Here I go lecturing . . . I understand you are going to be a doctor and work in a hospital. God knows India can do with doctors'. After a long pause Robin got up saying it was time he went to bed. 'It has been a long day for me and I must be fresh tomorrow'. He was nearing the door when he suddenly turned round, blew me a kiss, 'And if at times you find Maurice trying, do remember that his childish innocence is his most redeeming quality'.

Dr Sharma had likened the marriage of an Iengar with an Iyer to that of a white to a black American. What would he have said of ours? Iyers and Iengars shared a country, a mother tongue, a religion. Ours were different countries, different languages, different educational systems, different nursery rhymes, even our sense of humour and our religious beliefs were different. Compared with ours, a marriage across caste, let alone sub-caste, was positively incestuous. To rely upon sex alone to bridge the gap would have been folly.

During our honeymoon I made Maurice read Gabriel Chevallier's 'Clochemerle' as an introduction to aspects of French culture he could not have gathered from the complete works of Sainte-Beuve which he read, as he once wrote, 'for my sake'. It would, I realised, take time before he saw marriage my way. In the meantime I would try to understand him better and I plied him with questions about himself, his friends, life in India. I waited after a particularly satisfactory cuddle to ask about his ex-fiancée.

'She is a very nice girl, sweet-natured and gentle. I don't know why, but she took such a dislike to my friends that we began to quarrel and she broke it off. My friends did not approve because she is domiciled but they did not say anything against her. On the contrary, they tried to make her feel welcome. When one Collector I knew married a girl who was domiciled his Commissioner did not go to the wedding and he was transferred to an unpleasant district. They could not stop him getting married, and it did not damage his career. He now has one of the best jobs in the Province; but she has never forgotten the insult, though they have been happily married for years. It was she who told me the story.

'Thank God we are not like the Army where your fiancée has to be vetted by your Commanding Officer, or like the banks who forbid your getting married before thirty, and then they have to vet your bride. We can get married to whomsoever we like.'

Maurice sat up, pushed back the covers and repeated; 'I was quite cut up when she broke off our engagement. Actually got drunk for the first and only time.'

'How did it start?'

'We met at a party. She was very pretty. I offered to drive her home. In those days I had a car. We got talking about a film they were showing at the Regal cinema and I invited her to see it. After the film, as I was saying goodbye, she asked me why I had not kissed her. It was very embarrassing, so I kissed her. Having kissed her, naturally, I proposed.'

'Because you kissed her!'

'I enjoyed kissing her. But you need not be jealous.'

'What happened to her?'

'She married a dashing Naval officer. They are now in Ceylon, I believe.'

It was during that fortnight we spent in each other's undiluted company that I tried to get an idea of what the

ICS was really like. And even more important, what would be expected of me.

For his first year in India Maurice had been attached to an official one year his senior, with whom he lived and spent several months touring the District. During that year, as a Supernumerary Assistant Collector, his job was to watch and learn while his mentor visited villages, held open court, dealt with demands for remission of the land revenue, issued agricultural loans, sentenced criminals and enforced law and order over an area a third the size of Wales. They toured on horseback and lived in tents. In the rainy season, Maurice spent his time in the headquarters town, preparing for his Revenue examination, learning the language and hearing simple cases. After that, he got a subdivision of his own. There he had malaria sixteen times in two years.

'I drank a lot of quinine, wrapped myself in as many blankets as I could and sweated it out. The worst part was the shaking and the depression from quinine. Riding with malaria is most unpleasant. And I took to dreaming in Marathi, the local language, and waking up every time I didn't know a word. In the District, once I was on my own, there was only one British official and the nearest British girl was in the next District, fully half a day's drive away. To leave one's District one had to get permission from one's superior. My Collector was Ishvaran. He and his wife treated me like a son. You must meet the Ishvarans, and Purviz Damry, who held the next subdivision, and Hari Singh, the Forest Officer with whom I shared a bungalow for a whole year. Hari Singh has a genius for improvisation. Purviz is a Parsi, very cultured. They did not take him into the ICS because, as an undergraduate he had a passion for Greek vases and classical music. The interviewers thought he was a sissy. He got into the Provincial Service instead. He is a good example of how silly interviewers can be. He is one of the best shots in the Bombay Presidency, he has a large collection of tigers to his credit; so has Zarine, his wife.

He has a hair-raising story of going after a wounded tiger on foot when the grass was still tall, so that if the tiger lay in wait it would be invisible. Remember, I used to write about going to shoot with them. And Hari Singh is the one who invited me to accompany him on part of his honeymoon. He was nervous to be alone all the time with Muni. Muni is tiny and very, very beautiful. It is wonderful to watch the way she twiddles that bulky husband of hers around her little finger.'

Beside his attacks of malaria Maurice had spent six months in a plaster cast which began below the shoulders and ended above the knees. He had fallen from a horse, breaking a couple of vertebrae. This was in Bombay when he was in charge of Air Raid Precautions. He worked in hospital, flat on his back, holding his files above his head.

'That was nothing really. The only nasty bit, in due course, was the itching. It is very damp and hot in Bombay.' With a chest that hairy, it must have been torture with maggots under the cast.

'Did you not get sick-leave; were you not sent to the hills?'

'The war was on. I had the first three days off while the cast was drying. You must remember we were very short-handed. But it wasn't so bad. After a month I was allowed out of hospital. By then I could walk. The only problem was sitting down.' A carpenter made him a contraption so that he could work at his desk.

It was during one of those intimate moments of our honeymoon that Maurice had a sudden explosion. His grievance was so burning that, propping himself up against the pillows, he announced, out of the blue, voice ringing with pent-up indignation that, while the India Office was stuffed with dinosaurs, the idiocy of the Government of India had to be seen to be believed.

'Really, darling! Can you imagine? As Resident Under-Secretary in Bombay, that magnificent flat I wrote to you about, remember? That was a perk-cum-bribe. I had to be on duty twenty-four hours in the twenty-four in case secret coded messages arrived from the Government of India. As the flat was on top of the Secretariat messages could be rushed up at night without delay. When I went out Robin or Astad, who shared the flat, stood in for me. You might have thought that Delhi would have used code - especially since it was the same as that of the Allied Forces - only for matters of extreme importance. No. Not they! Nothing of the sort! Some messages were so trivial that one wondered why they were coded in the first place. We soon got quite good at deciding which could wait till morning. I shall never forget the night a very long message marked 'Top Secret' arrived. It took me from two o'clock till six to decipher it. And when I picked up the morning paper it was there as a press communiqué!'

The indignation glowing on my husband's face suddenly made way to childish mirth as he went on: 'You know something? You have beside you in this very bed, the man responsible for the Allies having to change one of their major codes. I swear I did not do it on purpose. Shortly after that communiqué I lost the book. We searched everywhere. I am dreadfully absent-minded. Mother used to say it was a good thing I was born with my head screwed on my neck, otherwise I would forget it somewhere. I could not, for the life of me, remember where I had put that code. Served them right, even if it was an accident.'

I had no difficulty believing him. Maurice's absent-mindeness is Himalayan. He had arrived from India with a tattered suitcase half-filled with heavy wooden shoe-trees and only one spare pair of shoes and an impressive collection of keys, mostly large and rusty. The key to the suitcase was not amongst them. Everything was rationed in England. Clothes could only be bought with coupons. Yet he had left his clothes in India, except for a few bush-shirts, unsuitable for London in Spring, and that dreadful suit he wore in

Liverpool - purchased second-hand from a very tall missionary - and a pair of grey cotton trousers issued to Air Raid Precaution Wardens in Bombay. Fortunately, on landing he had been given enough clothing coupons to buy the suit, the shirt and the tie in which we got married. The rest, from underwear to dinner jacket, had to be borrowed from relatives. Yet, despite his extreme absent-mindedness, Maurice never forgot a name, an address or a telephone number. So much so that he did not bother to jot them down.

4

Britain's Indians

Back in London from our honeymoon we got an invitation from one of Maurice's Indian colleagues.

'HVR Iengar belongs to the Bombay Cadre like myself. He is very senior and has come to England to accompany Sir Ardashir Dalal, the Member for Planning in the Viceroy's Executive Council. You will like 'HVR' - that's how he is called. He is an extremely nice man'.

That dinner in a private suite at the Savoy was an unforgettable introduction to the British Raj in India. Sir Ardashir Dalal was courtesy itself. Both he and HVR went out of their way to make me feel welcome. They took great care not to talk shop in a manner which cut me out. Whenever they used administrative jargonese, they translated it into plain English. Maurice talked to them freely. Both men were open-minded, ready to agree to some of his criticisms of the Government of India. When they disagreed, they explained why at length. My years with the informality of American academe had not prepared me for such staggering democracy.

Maurice later explained.

'You are right. England is a very hierarchical, an almost feudal society. But the ICS is different. There is of course the hierarchy of seniority but we are all part of the same cadre. We have been trained to see things in the same way and to act accordingly. HVR knows that one day I may have his job. He can still remember that when he was a young civilian his seniors listened to him much like parents listen to their bright child. What makes the ICS so special is the fluidity in the exchange of views. I was still in the District when I spent a few days in Delhi as Sir Jeremy Raiseman's guest. Sir Jeremy was then Finance Member the equivalent of the Chancellor of the Exchequer. I took the opportunity to tell him how things looked from my remote aboriginal area. He not only listened. He got a couple of Secretaries to the Government to listen and made them put down what I said in writing. The same thing happened when Lumley, the Governor of Bombay, came to my District. He was not ICS but he gave me three quarters of an hour after dinner and listened patiently to my plea that the War Effort could be made much more effective if only we could strike a deal with Congress. And he did point out the difficulties to me.

In India one's seniors listen. But make no mistake, being allowed to discuss and argue doesn't give one the licence to disobey orders. It is perfectly permissible to note one's views on the file, but one is not expected to resent being over-ruled. One has to carry out orders once they are given.'

Maurice went back to India shortly after VJ Day, leaving me behind despite my having been registered for a passage from England on the 1st of February (when I was still in America). I had been given priority number 1274 which, he wrote at the time, 'is not as bad as it sounds since I believe 800 to 900 of the 1274 have already come out. I have every hope there will be no difficulty about your coming back with me.' Instead I had to wait my turn to be allotted a passage by the Indian High Commission.

In my eagerness to follow as soon as possible I decided the best way to shorten the wait would be to pester the relevant officials.

Maurice had already told me that India Office was 'stuffed with dinosaurs. Would you believe it? - when I told one of the Principals of that Office that India would soon become independent he said India could *never* be given independence because Gurkha recruits to the Army have to come across India. What an idiot!' I had been warned against the India Office, but nothing Maurice said had prepared me for the Indian High Commission.

Inside a massive building guarded by two stone elephants I was directed to a queue in a corner of the impressive entrance hall. A row of chairs led to a door at the end of a corridor. I sat next to an elderly Indian impeccably dressed in pin-stripe with fawn-coloured spats and matching gloves carefully folded against the brim of the bowler-hat resting on his knees. He gave me a friendly smile and plunged back into *The Times.* There were half a dozen Indians before him. A grey-haired lady wrapped in a dark-green sari with a gold border was sitting at the head of the queue. Her crocodile handbag and her jewels proclaimed an affluence she in no way flaunted. In those days the Indians in England were usually people of position and education. I must have sat there for a quarter of an hour - two Indians had joined the queue - when a youngish man in a hurry spotted me. Deflecting his course he came over to enquire what I was waiting for.

'Move over!' he ordered the queue and, to my utter confusion, insisted on my taking the first chair, despite my protests. I said I had plenty of time and did not mind waiting.

'We British must uphold the Raj!' he snapped and vanished behind the door. I was called in almost immediately.

The white hair and sideburns, the pink cheeks and myopic blue eyes of the man behind the desk conjured up a guinea-pig, a likeness made more striking by a gap between his tobacco-stained front teeth.

'My Dear. I am so sorry. Had I known I would not have kept you waiting.' There was a tea-tray on the desk with the nibbled remains of a biscuit.

'What can I do for you?' He listened, made notes and explained there was a very long waiting list for non-priority passages to India because essential personnel and troops took precedence and that shipping space had been greatly reduced by sinkings during the war.

'It may take a year before your turn comes, but with luck it could be only a few months. But, you can rest assured I will do what I can to put your name ahead of the natives. What is your husband's job?' All I knew was that Maurice was Under-Secretary in the Ministry of Finance in Delhi and that his boss was called Sen Gupta.

'What! A native!' Sideburns awobble with indignation the guinea-pig extended his tobacco-stained freckled hand as if to pat me better. 'My poor child. How awful! I expect you will have to meet them socially and treat them as equals!'

The next time I ventured into the High Commission it was three months later to collect my passage. Had I been lucky? Had he kept his word? . . . Of one thing I was sure: Maurice had not pulled strings. It would have been totally out of character.

Maurice was waiting for me in Bombay.

When he saw the conditions in which I had travelled he exclaimed: 'Thank God it is you. Women are so much tougher than men.' He had gone first class with a cabin and a bathroom to himself. I had been crammed into a troop-ship carrying far more than its intended load. Had I not remembered that, under the jest, lay a deep-seated belief in the superiority of women, I might have been annoyed. It is to Maurice that Bombay owed its first female intake into the Administration. When he recruited as one of his Assistants in Air Raid Precautions Miss Salukhere, an orphaned Brahmin graduate with brothers to educate who later married an Ambassador, he had had to battle against the government's reluctance to employ women, except as switch-board operators. The very sight of a woman in the Secretariat, that wholly male domain - secretaries, typists, even tea-servers, used to be men - would, it was feared, distract staff. And what about facilities? By the time I reached India in October 1945 that prejudice had been eroded. There were women even in the Delhi Secretariat.

We stayed in Bombay. Time to catch up on each other. Time to meet some of Maurice's closest friends. Time to get a whiff of the real, as opposed to the official, India.

Our bedroom in Bombay Castle was huge. The bed stood on a woven mat. The mat, dead in the centre of the room, was there to reduce the cold between bare feet and the polished stone floor extending far away towards walls made to look even more remote by the extraordinary length of the electric flexes connecting the table-lamps on either side of the bed to their wall-sockets. Engulfed in a vast mosquito-net the bed was under a huge ceiling-fan suspended by a thirty-feet long rod.

Tactfully absent, our host had left on the bedside-tables a collation of exotic fruit and a thermos flask filled with the deliciously chilled juice of sweet limes. Except for the furnished island of that bed, the room was bare - forty feet by sixty of emptiness, thirty feet tall. Wardrobes, chests of drawers etc were tucked away in four small communicating rooms, away from huge gothic windows. There was at least one other room that huge. Like our bedroom. Only its centre, right under the ceiling fan, had been furnished as a drawing-room. The furniture was scattered around a central carpet: sofas, casual tables, chairs. That way they occupied more space, transforming the raft into an oasis complete with palms in glittering brass pots. Set in one of the alcoves of the drawing-room, the dining-room alone was to scale. It could sit twelve.

'Now my Darling, you see how it was possible for me to put up twenty people; there's oodles of room.'

'But what about beds?' Finding twenty beds could not be that easy.

'No problem. In India people travel with their bedding-rolls'. Maurice showed me his bedding-roll, a bulky khaki-coloured sausage laying in a corner of our dressing-room. 'We will get one for you. One keeps all one needs for a journey inside; sheets, blankets, pillows. There are pockets for wash-things, night-clothes, books . . . even towels. When one wants to sleep, one unties the straps and rolls it out. It makes a very comfortable bed.'

Johnny Bowman, our host, a year Maurice's junior, appeared next morning for breakfast.

'Welcome to India! If only you knew how relieved we all were when he got married. For years Maurice had been boring us with your merits, he was positively obsessed. We kept telling him to propose, but he kept saying it would not be fair on such scanty acquaintance and that he was afraid you would turn him down.'

'Sunny Boy' flashed through my mind as I listened to that tall, slim, blue-eyed Scot.

'Raoji!' Johnny yelled. Barefooted, beturbanned, clasped inside a cummerbund far too broad, a servant appeared. 'Khana lao!' (Bring the food.) 'Let's have breakfast. I am starving. Have been downstairs already for a couple of hours. I like to get as much work done as possible before it gets too hot.'

'Excellent idea. Then you can have a siesta after lunch'.

'A siesta. My dear Taya, siestas are for the ladies. During the week no siesta for us, only on Sundays and on public holidays . . . and even then only if all the work is done.'

'When I was in the West Indies, in the Dominican Republic and in Haiti, many Europeans worked from seven in the morning till two in the afternoon.' Maurice and Johnny spoke at the same time: 'That would not do.' They worked the whole of Saturday and would never leave the office without clearing urgent files, no matter how long it might take.

'I consider myself lucky if I finish in time to have a

leisurely bath before dinner. Dinner, I expect you know, is late. Never before nine, usually around ten, sometimes later. Drinks start at sunset.' Waving to Maurice, Johnny chuckled: 'Remember that Naval Captain we put up, the one with DTs who kept the blinds down so that he could pretend it was sunset in the morning? Remember the night we had to rescue him from an imaginary rat invasion? . . . By the way, Taya. I hope you won't mind my leaving Maurice to show you round. He's an old Bombay-wallah and I have a lot of work. Keep Sunday free. I want to show you a bit of our countryside and I have booked the Salt Collector's Bungalow at Marve. We will take a picnic. All you need to bring is bathing costumes. In the meantime make yourself at home. Anything you need just ask Raoji; all you have to do is call him.' Despite the size of the flat there were no bells. One had to yell. Good servants always remain within earshot. Like shadows, they glide noiselessly, destroying privacy. In time I became so used to their ubiquitous presence that, as with furniture, I ceased to be aware of their existence.

After breakfast we went to the docks to clear my luggage through customs. Maurice took the opportunity to call on the Collector of Customs who went out of his way to impress upon me the Service attitude. His lecture would have sounded pompous had it not been for his obvious love of India.

'They look to us for justice and fair-play. Always remember that if a man is poor and illiterate it does not mean that he is stupid or bad and it most certainly does not give anyone the right to push him about. The Indian masses are exploited not by us but by the Indians themselves. Beside the money-lenders there is the caste system; it gives the higher castes an excuse to oppress the lower castes. We are here to see that justice is done without fear or favour, that Untouchable and Brahmin are equal before the law. To be in the ICS is an honour, a great privilege which has to be earned by proper conduct. Never forget, wherever you are, that in the eyes of the people you represent the King Emperor. But I am sure that Maurice has already explained all that.' He had. I could not help feeling that the Collector of Customs was laying it on unnecessarily thick. At no time had Maurice mentioned the King Emperor. On the contrary. In a letter answering my questions, a letter I knew practically by heart he had written:

'An ICS wife has no duties or restrictions beyond those of a decent citizen. In fact she has less than most. She is at the top, or nearly, of local society. She can therefore know anybody she wants without being thought a social climber or risking to lose her position. A large proportion of the people we know will be officials, ICS, Police, Medical, Forest or Army. Most of the rest will be big business. Many of our friends will be richer - in my job you meet many of India's millionaires, and some one naturally likes. In India life on the cheap is impossible. So many of the overheads are expensive: rent, servants, entertaining, a car . . . Government does not approve of its senior servants living below a certain level because it reduces their contacts, usefulness and efficiency. Beside the officials and big business there will also be a few journalists and politicians. Fortunately politics do not affect social relations much. One of the nicest congratulations on our engagement came from Mrs Pandit, Nehru's sister.'

He had never mentioned I would have to represent the King Emperor. This, I was to discover to my dismay, had been oversight. Or was it? Maybe it was because he knew I was a foreigner that he had written in another letter: 'the number of people an ICS Pool Officer really has to watch his step with is very small. So you won't have to be careful more than once a week or a fortnight. Actually our seniors are very reasonable people with a social conscience. With those who do not have such a social conscience, the Army and business mainly, you can be as rude as you like. It is only for my own Service that I have the deepest respect. The Service does mean a great deal to me. Any adjustment to it that you make I will appreciate very much. Otherwise go your own way. Being French is a great advantage. It puts you outside all India's racial fights: Hindu-Muslim, Indian-English, even Indian-English-American, Brahmin-non-Brahmin . . . The French tradition of judging a man by his standards, and not by his colour or creed, will stand you in very good stead. Race prejudice is the worst of all Indian poisons.' Not a word about my being a reincarnation of the King Emperor.

'Did he really mean that about the King Emperor?'

'Well, yes. In a sense all of us represent Britain. That is why you will not find a British down-and-out in India; he would be repatriated. We have an image to uphold. We are discouraged from retiring in India because we are here to serve, not colonise. Setting the example is expected of the ICS. Noblesse oblige. Even in my first year, when I visited a village, I was preceded by a runner shouting 'Sarkar Yetat,' 'The Government is coming.' Heady stuff, don't you think, for one fresh out of university? But don't worry, Darling. You have the making of a perfect Memsahib.' Staunchly republican, meritocratic, and anti-colonialist, what Maurice obviously meant as a compliment felt like a slap. I remained silent the twenty minutes it took us to walk back to the Secretariat. 'Memsahib' had such a nasty ring.

5

The jewel in India's crown

That week in Bombay, crammed to bursting with first impressions, remains branded in my memory.

First, we had lunch with the Symingtons. Maurice's first year as an apprentice had been with David, for whom he had the adoration of a child for his teacher, an adoration which extended to Anne, David's wife. He had sung their praise so often that I was quite nervous. Would I do? It did not seem to cross Maurice's mind that I might feel apprehensive. In the car they sent for us he explained that David was Secretary to the Governor of Bombay, a very senior post.

'His house on Nepean Road has a unique view of the bay. Anne is a genius at interior decoration, not surprising since she studied Art in London. She is very much looking forward to meeting you and I know you will simply love each other.'

A tall and handsome couple welcomed us as the car pulled to. Maurice had been right. The view from Malabar Point across the bay was fantastic, far more impressive than Promenade des Anglais.

'Beautiful, isn't it?' said Anne; 'at night, when it is lit up now that the black-out is over, thank God, it is magnificent. We call it the Queen's necklace. We are indeed lucky to be near HE'. What did she mean by 'HE'? It did not take me long, from her conversation, to work out that 'HE' and 'Her X' meant His and Her Excellencies, the Governor of Bombay and his wife.

Maurice had been right about Anne's gift for interior decoration. Everything in the house was pefect; the chintz of the curtains, the flowers, the table napkins skilfully folded to look like peacocks, the service, the food. Everything had been orchestrated with harmony. Not one discordant note. Not a single lapse. So what was it that made me so uncomfortable? Was it the uniform of the bearer hovering over us to refill glasses, splendid in Government House regalia, red and gold on a dazzling white which darkened his features? Or was it the sudden conviction that Anne was the perfect Memsahib - a memsahib as English as kippers? Even the tiger-rug with its stuffed head looked British. In my Frenchness I realized that I could never be a perfect Memsahib.

After lunch we walked over to the Rocky Hill Flats. Perched above the sea on Malabar Hill, they were for junior Government servants.

'You will like them, I know. We are in luck. It's a public holiday, so the husbands will be at home. All my friends are dying to meet you.' They welcomed me with open hearts.

The wives were, with a few exceptions, incredibly beautiful. The grace with which they moved. The elegant flow of their saris. The lustre of their hair. The velvet of their big eyes. The cinnamon of their skin and the smallness of their bones. I felt gross with my stumpy fingers and wide waist. I watched with fascination Joan Dias play with gold bangles only fit for a small European child. As if made of rubber, she kept shaping her hands into cornets. Her slender wrists ended in tapering fingers as she threaded her bangles up and down while she talked. Vivacious, Joan spoke very fast, in staccato bursts, with that enchanting lilt, accompanying her words with little side movements of the head. The slight bulge of her eyes lent its sheen to a child-like eagerness full of charm. How different from Lily Nadkarni's perfect beauty, a beauty radiating an infectiously serene contentment. Lily spoke deliberately, moved slowly like some ancient goddess. 'How lucky her husband must be,' I thought. Lily was by far the fairest of them all.

We, the women, sat down. The men stood in a corner. This, I subsequently discovered to my annoyance, was customary. Neither France nor America had prepared me for the sex-segregation so frequently practised in England and India.

Later I plied Maurice with questions.

'Why does Tony Dias have blue eyes? I thought all Indians have brown eyes.' 'Joan and Tony come from Goa.* Between Goan Christians and the Portuguese there has been inter-marriage.' So that explained the gold cross on Joan's neck. It had puzzled me. I did not expect to find Christians in India.

'Is that why Lily is so fair?'

'Good heavens, no! Lily is not a Goan. She is a Saraswat Brahmin, like her husband. Brahmins can be very fair.'

'So it was an arranged marriage?'

'No. As a matter of fact it was a most unusual love match. Lily's father is a Police Deputy Superintendent promoted from Sub-Inspector. And she had no dowry. Indian ICS officers are much sought after and command very large dowries. No. It was love at first sight. Lily is so nice that everybody was delighted.'

'Why were they all making so much fuss about how lucky that great hulk of a man with the tiny wife was? Why did they keep saying it was a miracle he was alive?'

'You mean Fateh Singh Rana? Didn't you hear him say he was mauled by a tiger when the villagers in his district asked him to kill their man-eater?' I had heard.

'Yes, he said he had wounded the beast but did not have time to reload, and had to free himself with bare hands when the beast jumped on him. But it can't have been very difficult. He said himself the tiger was very old and prac-

*Tony Dias later became Governor of Bengal.

tically toothless.' Maurice explained that survivors of tiger attacks usually die of blood-poisoning because the claws are infectious.

'You heard Fateh Singh say that Allah must have been with him that day.'

When I asked Maurice why all his friends, with the exception of the Symingtons, had identical furniture; same tables, same chairs, same sofas, same standard lamps, he laughed.

'It is not their furniture. You see, Darling, in our Service one is liable to be transferred all the time. So Government provides furnished accommodation. We have to pay rent, of course, ten percent of our pay, and there is a kind of scale laying down what furniture one is entitled to, depending on position.'

Our last call in the Rocky Hill Flats had been to the Wagles. At the top of the stairs we were greeted by a cherub with dark curls, huge black eyes enlarged by thick, long, turned up lashes.

'Mummy! Mummy! They have arrived!' It was two-year-old Asha, Premy's daughter.

'She's been so excited, waiting to see you,' said her mother. 'Welcome to India, my dear.' Premy's voice was free from that soft lilt, reminder she had been to St Paul's. She was, in some indefinable way, very different from the Indian wives I had met that afternoon. Fateh Singh Rana's tiny wife, like Kala and Sushila, was traditional. Lily was modern. Joan was westernized. Premy was western.

Tall, slim, elegant, Premy in her slacks could have stepped out of a page of *Vogue*, preferably a page devoted to sportswear. Nitya, a contemporary of Maurice's in the Service, was unmistakably Indian. Darkly handsome he had the quiet arrogance I came to associate with Maharashtrian Brahmins, but he had it in greater degree. Unlike Nitya, Premy looked out of place in that govenment-furnished flat.

'Darlings, we are going to meet again tonight for dinner, so I won't keep you long. Taya must be exhausted. Meeting so many people all at once, Maurice, my pet, you should take her back for a good rest. My parents won't expect you before nine. There will be the old crowd: the Wadias, the Baigs, the Hutteesinghs and Sir Francis Low. Taya, get Maurice to give you the low-down and do bring a shawl or something. It gets pleasantly cool in October and we usually sit out in the garden for coffee.'

'Premy's father is a very senior member of our Service. He was India's Deputy High Commissioner in London before the war. Now he is Chairman of the Bombay Port Trust. Lady Rama Rau, his wife, is a staunch supporter of the Congress and an active feminist. The Wadias are among India's nicest millionaires. Neville is a Christian Parsi. The family owns Bombay Dyeing, one of India's largest textile firms. His wife Dina is Jinnah's only child. She and Premy are great friends. But Darling, you must not mention Jinnah to her. You see, Jinnah is a fanatic. He disowned his daughter because she did not marry a Muslim. Yet he himself did not marry a Muslim. Dina's mother was a Parsi. She was very beautiful and much younger. Jinnah fell in love and swept her off her feet. It was not a happy marriage. She committed suicide on her thirtieth birthday because she was afraid of getting old. Dina inherited her mother's fortune and is a millionairess in her own right. Both Neville and Dina are very nice.' As instructed, Maurice was giving me the low-down.

'Rashid Baig is the Sheriff of Bombay. He is a Muslim. His wife Tara is a half-American, half-Bengali Hindu and the Hutteesinghs are Hindus. Raja is a Gujerati mill-owner and a staunch Congressman. He has spent years in jail because of Gandhi's non-cooperation. His wife Betty is Nehru's younger sister.'

'Did she go to jail too?'

'No, Betty is not really interested in politics. Sir Francis Low is the editor of the *Times of India*. It is British-owned.'

That evening at the Rama Rau's remains unforgettable. Not because of the exalted company, the delicious food or the elegant setting, but because of the turn the conversation took over coffee in the garden. As the arguments went round, back and forth, I listened, amazed.

They were discussing what would happen now that the war was over and the Congress was no longer in jail. Would the British leave and grant India the independence Gandhi demanded? What about Jinnah's Pakistan? Rashid Baig was agreeing with Sir Rama Rau that it was all a political ploy. Hindus and Muslims were Indians. There was no reason why they should not continue to live together in peace after the British went.

'Jinnah is making all that fuss because Nehru pricked his vanity,' Rashid announced. 'Remember, he had retired from the Congress to practise law in England where he had a house in Hampstead and was minting money at the Bar. Then some idiot repeated to him that Nehru said: "Jinnah is finished." So to teach Nehru a lesson, he chucked his practice, sold his house, rushed back to India, plunged into sectarian politics, put teeth into the moribund Muslim League and asked for the creation of Pakistan. All that, just to show Nehru that he was not finished! Ask Dina if I am inventing.' Dina lit a cigarette, nodded and began to blow smoke-rings with enviable skill. Thus encouraged, Rashid went on: 'It's all a farce, Jinnah drinks, and he smokes. He does not know Arabic or even Urdu. He cannot read the Koran. He is an agnostic, not a Muslim. And like Gandhi he is a Gujerati. What claim does he have to represent the Muslims? I tell you, he has none.'

This sounded so ominously like conversations I had heard in the thirties that I could not help interjecting.

'Hitler was not German,' to which Lady Rama Rau protested.

'The situation is *quite* different. To get Pakistan Jinnah

would have to create the conditions for a war of religion and religious wars are things of the past, like Crusades. We are not in the Middle-Ages, we are in the twentieth century. People are far too civilised to go to war for differences of religion. Rioting, yes. I grant you that sometimes people get killed because of music before mosques or because cows are slaughtered. But civil-war and a country carved up because of religion, most certainly not. Who has heard of such a thing in the twentieth century!'

'What about Ireland?' Maurice asked. Everybody began, at once, to explain that India was different.

Raja Hutteesingh blamed Jinnah's success with the Muslim League on the British.

'Divide and Rule is the British motto. You hope that if we can't agree between ourselves you will be able to stay forever and continue to exploit us. India is not the Jewel of your Crown for nothing.'

'I don't feel exploited', Nitya said. Neither did Rashid, nor Sir Rama Rau. But his wife and Raja kept insisting that India would be rich were it not for British exploitation. Both of them agreed with Rashid that the Hindu-Muslim problem was a British creation which Jinnah had been encouraged to exploit because it retarded an eventual hand-over.

Everybody's refusal to admit the importance of religion and Maurice's and Sir Francis Low's lack of concern when they were being attacked, struck me as extraordinary.

In France, religion is a matter of crucial importance, whether one is for it or against it. So important, in fact, that I was taught as a child never to enquire which religion people belonged to or how much they earned. I had not forgotten the massacres following the Revocation of the Edict of Nantes. Religious genocide is part of French lore. Politics, too, were a slippery subject of conversation.

'Why should I take offence? I am used to England being criticised. It does not interfere with friendships. Indians are always very careful to make clear that they are criticising

England, not one personally.' Maurice added that arresting people did not lead to personal resentment. 'Take Robin. It was he who arrested Morarji Desai and kept him in jail during the war. Morarji has the highest opinion of Robin. And when Nehru's father was in jail it is said the Governor of the UP not only sent him champagne but made it a point to instruct the warden to have it chilled.'

'Amazing! We, in France, take politics even more seriously than religion.'

The extent to which politics can be divisive in France as they never seem to be in England was demonstrated to Maurice during the Algerian war when one of my cousins ceased to be on speaking terms with her only son because he took opposite sides. So, naturally, I was amazed listening to our hostess. For the wife of a senior administrator to openly criticise the Government made my imagination boggle.

'Sir Rama Rau must be retired.'

'Of course not!' Such naiveté earned me a fond smile. 'If he were retired he would not live in that mansion on Cumballa Hill. He could not afford it. The Port Trust House is far more beautiful than the Wadia house, though they are multi-millionaires. No. He is not retired. Like the Governor of the Reserve Bank, he is entitled to a house which is second only to that of the Governor.'

The Chairman of the Port Trust's residence was indeed splendid. Vast, on two floors, with a beautiful garden and a fleet of impeccably starched servants, gliding bare-foot on marble floors. The open colonnade at the end of the terrace where we sat for coffee was vaguely reminiscent of Pompeii. Backed against the last pillar, a large floodlit bronze statue flayed the air with four arms, perilously perched on one foot.

'The original is in the Madras Museum. Our best dancing Shiva. Twelfth century. You *must* get Maurice to take you South.' Lady Rama Rau smiled approvingly as I admired her God.

Exceedingly handsome, tall, statuesque, superb body, suggested rather than revealed, she looked like Juno. Ancient goddess, she was draped in dark red silk with a wide gold brocade border flowing behind her back, firmly anchored to her shoulder by a large discus of chiselled rubies. The other ladies, despite their saris and their complexion, looked much less Indian. Imported French georgette, printed or embroidered, was the craze. Fashion excluded the kind of fastening which was Lady Rama Rau's hallmark. Lady Rama Rau alone had a bun. Fashion was to short hair. She alone did not wear make-up or modern jewelry.

Curled in a big arm-chair Dina was bristling with diamonds. An emerald-cut solitaire dwarfed her expressive hand. More striking than the size of that sparkler was the way she moved, vivacious quicksilver, in sharp contrast to her handsome husband's quiet calm. A marriage of extremes. No wonder they had been attracted to each other.

6

The belles of Bombay

I met so many people, saw so many things in so short a time that my impressions, if vivid, are confused. Which of Maurice's friends took us to the Races? Was it Neville Wadia, or was it Sonny Habibullah, one of the Taluqdars of Oudh, a keen horse-breeder? His wife, it was said, was so beautiful that there were only two things one could not afford to miss seeing in India: the Taj Mahal and Atiyah's eyes. She was talented too and later became a writer under her maiden name of Hussein. Sonny was helping the Government of India to run textile control. Atiyah, with those eyes, needed no jewelry.

In 1945 oriental ostentation flowered at the Races. The display of wealth in the Members' Enclosure was so fabulous that it dwarfed everything, except a Coronation. Princes in gold brocades, dripping with jewelry, strutting, peacock-like. And the women! . . . Georgette saris littered with embroidery of silver, gold and precious stones. A beautiful woman in a flimsy pale-pink sari covered with arabesques in seed pearls was deep in conversation with Premy. By the time we joined Premy, she had gone. Who was that beauty?

'You mean Ayesha Cooch-Bihar? She *is* lovely. We became friends in England.' The next time I saw that beautiful creature she was in slacks. It was half a dozen years later. By then I was the correspondent of the *Manchester*

Guardian and the *Economist* and she the Maharajah of Jaipur's number three wife.

The display of wealth I was privileged to witness at the Bombay Races is a thing of the past. Ostentation on such a grand scale has been swept away by the Transfer of Power from Britain to the Indian National Congress. Their Highnesses, pensioned off, lived in fear of an avowedly Socialistic Pattern of Democracy. In the fifteen years I spent in India I only saw another display of wealth comparable to that of the Bombay Races when the daughter of the Maharajah of Gwalior was married in the mid-fifties. Casting prudence to the wind, Their Highnesses turned out in full regalia as if to cock a last fling at the sham Gandhian austerity of their new masters.

We spent our last day with Johnny. He had reserved the Salt Collector's Bungalow, a handsome wooden structure on a selected sandy beach shaded by coconut trees. In those days Bombay, which had perhaps two million people, ended at Nariman Point and the twenty odd miles of suburbia to Marve were generously peppered with paddy fields, coconut groves and thatched huts which reminded me of the West Indies. The main difference was an endless row of stables for water-buffaloes, those ugly beasts which, Maurice said, supplied Bombay with milk. The buffalo-keepers slept above the stables as if suspended in mid-air, their belongings dangling in the breeze.

Before leaving Bombay we went to pick up Malati.

'She is quite a girl,' Johnny said. 'Maurice, you of course know her father, Sir JP the Food Member. In her own way she is a chip off the old block. Studies at the Tata Institute; wants to have a career.' We stopped at the Institute's hostel and waited for Johnny who soon emerged with Malati.

Piquante, petite, with big black-eyes, a fine patrician nose, dazzling white teeth made whiter by the café crème of her skin. Malati was all abubble. Head never still, she kept shaking the silky red-black curls which framed the expressive oval of her face with their halo shimmering in the light. She was quite unlike the Indian women I had met so far . . . she lacked their stillness . . . she was exuberant with an optimistic dynamism which was infectious. She climbed in the car, flicked her sandals to the floor and sat cross-legged beside me, toes tucked under her knees. In her white cotton sari she looked fresh, full of kittenish vitality.

'Maurice, Johnny has told me so many stories about the days when you shared a flat that I have been dying to meet you. Is it true that he once shaved a V for victory on your chest while you were asleep?'

'I was not asleep. Far from it. He got Astad and Robin to hold me down. It looked awful, and as it grew it itched.'

By the time we reached our destination Malati had told me that she had been in Bombay nearly a year, that hers was the first batch of Social Science students and that she was in revolt against her parents.

'Daddy wants to marry me off before I am twenty. Not me, no Sir! I am a career girl. If I get married it will not be an arranged marriage like Mummy's. Mummy, poor darling, was married as a child. I want to be independent, work and earn my living.' Her mother had wept at the prospect of her youngest daughter being on her own in Bombay. '"Who will marry you after such scandalous behaviour?" she kept asking me. When I explained that I would live in a girls' hostel she backed me against Daddy. But first I had to promise that I would not eat beef, come what may. Mummy, of course, is a vegetarian. I eat everything, except beef. And because she is afraid I might starve, she keeps sending me food. Poor Mummy.'

We had arrived. Johnny suggested a swim before lunch and Malati took me inside to change. The furniture was spartan. The same as Johnny's and that of the Rocky Hill Flats.

'Does everybody in India have the same furniture?' I asked.

'It's PWD furniture.' Malati laughed and added that the

PWD looked after Government Servants from the cradle to the grave.

'What is PWD?'

'It is the Public Works Department. They will even come to mend your tap or change an electric bulb. But you can't expect imagination from a government department, only efficiency as Daddy keeps saying.' Malati had begun to unwind her sari. I asked her to demonstrate how to put on a sari. She showed me and made me try a couple of times until I got the hang of it. Then she confessed that she frequently cheated. 'I pin the pleats at the waist and on my shoulder with safety-pins when I go to work or to dance. I love dancing. Don't you? By the way, poor Mummy had quite a fit when two of my elder sisters, Sarala and Shanki insisted on learning Indian dancing. That was their form of revolt. Indian dancing is an ancient art but it is performed by temple prostitutes. No respectable Indian woman, with the exception of Mrinalini Sarabhai, who has her troupe of dancers, dances in public. Only temple dancers and ex-prostitutes do. My sisters had to promise they would never dance in public for money, unless it was for charity. It is different for Mrinalini Sarabhai. She is not a Kayastha. Besides, the Sarabhais are Gujeratis, Gandhians and very eccentric, not like us who are from the U P. Mummy and Daddy would *die* if Sarala or Shanki danced for money!' As we sat on the beach Malati, who had a lovely voice, sang Western songs.

We splashed in the water, Malati and Johnny went off on their own. 'Are they lovers?' I asked Maurice.

'What an idea. Don't be ridiculous! Indian society is very old-fashioned. It would be very, very wrong of Johnny to take advantage. I think they are in love. I suppose one of these days they will get married.' Maurice was wrong. But they are still close friends and Malati has her career. She is the Secretary of the Breach Candy Hospital, Bombay's best.

The extent to which the Indian Civil Service was all-embracing seared itself on my mind. Even now, whenever I think about India, it is in ICS terms despite the fact that I was an ICS wife for two years only. Invisible, yet tangible like the filaments of a man of war, the ICS cast its net and trapped me in the short span of that week. The Collector of Customs had been right. I, a French Republican anti-colonialist, had been turned into a Memsahib burdened by the realisation that I, too, was a representative of the King Emperor. Upon me had fallen, absurd, ridiculous as it was, a fraction of the British Raj. Not until India became independent could I be irresponsible again.

During that first week in India I was profoundly impressed by the total lack of racism which welded the British and Indian elements into that 'Steel Frame' as the ICS proudly dubbed itself. What a contrast to the United States where negros - as blacks were then called - were kept at bay: separate seats, separate benches, separate hotels, even in New York. I had been refused service because a Haitian friend was with me. In India, as far as I was able to observe, harmony reigned amongst Maurice's friends, be they Hindus, Muslims, Parsees or Christians, inside and outside the Service. Was it the arranging of marriages which, by preventing inter-marriage, made social mixing possible in a way unthinkable in worlds threatened by the solvent of love? Love marriages were still so much the exception in India, that rather than heralding change, they confirmed the rule.

I had been so busy in Bombay that I did not notice those contrasts between rich and poor which, very soon and to Maurice's annoyance, convinced me of the futility of British Rule. He, too, thought British Rule obsolete, but he was proud of what he felt sure would be Britain's legacy after independence, a legacy which would justify the imperialist past. My quarrel with him was to be about the lack of hospitals, schools and English-speakers in rural India. When I visited Senegal in 1938, at the end of a narrow gauge railway line, in a God-forsaken place called, I think, Bargnigoudouff, everybody spoke pigeon-French and there was a dispensary as well as a school. In village India hardly anybody spoke English and dispensaries were very rare. But, during that first week I was blind. I did not notice Bombay's slums and my first introduction to people living rough was at the railway station as we wended our way to the Punjab Mail heading for Delhi.

An architectural solecism, its baroquely ornate gothic facade clashing with its tropical surroundings, the station was everything Kipling's Kim led me to expect. The crowds. The smells. The din. The bustle. It was as if all India, but for its cattle, had congregated under a cathedral-shaped glass canopy. Infants, children, women, beggars, pie-dogs, cooking pots, earthen-jars, brass buckets, bedding-rolls, bundles. Red turbanned porters with huge brass number-plates gleaming against red cotton shirts, balanced heavy loads on their heads, carrying extra loads under their arms, tight-rope acrobats slicing forward through dense crowds. Travellers, sleepers and vendors, packed the platforms. 'Chaie garum, garum char', bellowed tea-vendors. 'Channa, channa', screamed roasted chick-peas vendors trying to drown the powerful snores of the steam engines.

I could barely believe my eyes. A woman squatting on her heels was actually cooking. With a wooden stick she was stirring a reddish stew in an earthen pot anchored between live embers, there, on the railway platform, surrounded by luggage, bundles and babies. Nobody seemed to mind. Barefoot, perilously near to the red hot embers, an old woman lay, face covered by the dirty corner of her sari, fast asleep. Kim's beloved Grand Trunk Road was camping in Victoria Station.

'They have no sense of time. Sometimes they arrive a whole day before their train is due. So they camp,' Maurice said, as we threaded our way towards the air-conditioned carriage.

Malati had come with Johnny to see us off. She hung a beautiful garland round my neck. It had a heart-shaped pendant of purple velvet embroidered with gold sequins saying 'WELCOME'. Johnny gave me a bouquet of strongly scented white flowers hallowed with fine silver threads.

'Raoji has got your compartment ready. I told him not to make the beds; you should sit up and look out till it gets dark. Taya, the run as far as Igatpuri is very picturesque. It goes through the Ghats. Raoji will have unpacked Maurice's toiletry in the bath-room and prepared cold drinks. The railway attendant will make your beds at Deolali, when he brings your dinner.' And he added 'if I were you I would get out at Deolali and stretch your legs. See if there are people you know on the train.'

Maurice said the names of first class passengers are displayed near the door of their compartment, for all to see.

'It is very useful. There may be someone you want to meet. That can save your having to make the trip. And if you are alone, it helps enliven the journey. There is often someone you know. As you will find out, India may be a huge country, but Indian society is very small. It is practically impossible to remain incognito, one nearly always meets an acquaintance.'

First class consisted of carriages with entirely self-contained compartments. No corridor or communicating door. Once the doors to the platform had been closed one was cut off from the rest of the world. The compartment with its own bathroom, WC and shower was most comfortable, with plenty of room for luggage. Being air-conditioned it was sealed off and free from soot or dust.

The view of the Western Ghats ranks ahead of America's Monument Valley because, unlike the decor of so many Westerns, the Ghats are not barren. Waterfalls, pools and the monsoon keep the gorges verdant, a lush background for spectacular rock formations which tower above the tropical forest.

Of that journey which lasted a day and a half I remember practically nothing, not even the Ghats, absorbed as we were in a renewed honeymoon made the more memorable by the gentle rocking of the train. Except for that blissful memory I recall a fleeting glimpse of the dappled shape of a panther stretching herself over the fork of a tree, the only big wild cat I managed to see during the fifteen years India was my home.

7

A rogue and some friends

As the train pulled into Delhi, dusk began to snuff out the sun so fast that it was already pitch dark when we left the station. Perched on a two-wheeled horse-drawn buggy, backs to the driver, feet atop luggage, chins knocking against knees, shaken like dice in that contraption Maurice said was a tonga, we set off. The driver kept clicking his tongue and his whip and abusing the beast's ancestry. I watched row after row of dimly lit bungalows vanish in the night. Deeply moved, I kept silent.

I was embarking on married life. *Home* was awaiting me at the end of that uncomfortable drive. Until now I had not felt married. Life with Maurice had been unreal, patchy, more like an affair. Free from responsibility, I had been on parade, in hotels, or a guest of his family and friends. In the six months we had been married we had not been together three. Not once had I made breakfast, taken a decision or been in charge. What kind of life lay ahead?

India was to be home for the rest of our active lives. Would I fit in? How soon would I be able to complete my studies and practise medicine? India was short of doctors and I was dying to get back into a hospital to pursue my vocation. With luck, from what Maurice had written, it should not take more than a year or two. Hospital work and research had been my goal from the age of six. After the Fall of Paris I had continued to study medicine, first in Toulouse, then in Haiti. In America, where I only had to study for another year to qualify, the quota for women's admission to Medical School meant that I had to wait till 1947 to enrol. That is why, instead, I had been working for a PhD in Biochemistry, with the understanding that in my final year I would get an MD as well. The subject of my research - pernicious anaemia in rats - was sufficiently related to medicine to get me in through the back door. By 1947 I would get two degrees instead of one and be a doctor, at last. However, at Maurice's insistence, I had left Madison to qualify in India. Since Biochemistry had been a *pis-aller*, I had not bothered to collect a Masters Degree, mere formality on the way to a PhD. How would Delhi's Medical School compare with Paris and Haiti? How would I combine studying and marriage? I snuggled closer to Maurice and looked at the unfamiliar stars - everything was going to be new. It was up to me to meet the challenge. I heard myself muttering Mother's parting words: 'Remember, marriage is what you make it.'

'We are nearly there, Darling. See those lights. It's the entrance to the Club. Sheikh Hussein must be waiting.' Maurice began to direct the tonga towards our quarters. Jumping from the tonga he helped me down. Sheikh Hussein was standing to attention, a floral garland in readiness for me.

'Salaam Memsahib. Much Welcome.' Then he busied himself with the luggage.

In the bedroom, beside Maurice's bed, a camp-bed had been prepared.

'What's that for?' Maurice asked.

'That, Sahib,' explained the bearer in all seriousness, 'is Memsahib's bed, of course.' As he took it away I heard him mutter loudly, 'in case Sahib tired need rest.'

Home, at the Imperial Delhi Gymkhana Club, consisted of two small communicating rooms, a bath-room and a tiny verandah chock-a-block with Maurice's trunks, tea-chests and camping-gear - the accretions of years touring the district. Hitherto space had not been a problem. He had been entitled to vast government accommodation. And, after his transfer to the Finance and Commerce Pool in Delhi, he had been a paying-guest with senior administrators residing in very spacious bungalows, usually with guest-suites attached. Because I had refused to start our life together as a paying-guest in somebody else's house, he had, in anticipation of a married quarter falling vacant, moved into bachelor accommodation in the Club. His name was well up the waiting list for the C-Class house to which he was entitled but there was an acute housing shortage in Delhi. There was no knowing how long it would take for a C-Class house to fall vacant.

In Bombay I had been told that, like all Western brides, I would get rid of Maurice's bearer. Had Sheikh Hussein been an angel - which I very soon discovered he was far from being - he would have resented me. Used to one master he now had two. Mistresses are more demanding than masters, and since they do not work, are at home a lot. Not that my presence bothered Sheikh Hussein unduly. He had a knack for disappearing shortly after Maurice went to his office and reappearing just in time to greet him home. Living as we did in a club, the bearer's duties were limited. He brought us bed-tea and the newspapers in the morning, ran our baths, made the bed, served drinks when we did not entertain in the common rooms, looked after Maurice's clothes, ran errands and supervised the club sweeper.The sweeper, being Untouchable, confined his attention to the floor and the WC. Dusting was not his job. For the first couple of days it was I who dusted. I can still see Sheikh Hussein's contemptuous grin as he watched me dust. Encouraged by the conviction that the Sahib had married a fool, he made the mistake of pointing out that I had forgotten to dust the mantelpiece. He dusted from then on.

Slim, fairly tall, rusty brown, he looked like a Red Indian.

Instead of feathers he wore a fez; oily wisps of hair dyed red escaped from the fez's greasy rim. Perhaps it was the aquiline nose, the small shiny eyes and the thin lips which reminded me of those scalping villains of the almanacks of my childhood. His tongue, dark orange from the chewing of betel, darted through a gap in decaying tobacco-stained teeth. The smell of tobacco, sweat and heavily scented hair-oil surrounded him. His nails were in perpetual mourning for the brushing they deserved. His coat, brown like the rest of him, stopped below the hips to expose shirt-tails of indefinable colour, hanging over dirty striped pyjamas.

To pretend I liked him would be hypocritical. In fairness, he had his strong points. He was a genuine artist at floral arrangements. Twice a week one of the Club gardeners left an armful of cut flowers on our doorstep. Fragrant sweet-peas, waxy cannas, marigolds, flame of the forest, roses, dark red sponge-like coxcombs, irises, anything in season, all pell-mell, and foliage. I am hopeless with flowers. Not so Sheikh Hussein. Without a moment's hesitation he would create bouquets worthy of Dutch or Florentine masters. His ironing was perfect and his packing of clothes professional. Yet, professionalism with clothes had not stopped him from packing a cooking pot inside Maurice's top-hat and ruining his riding boots by stuffing them with kitchen implements. His talents did not make up for his sloth, filth and dishonesty. After I caught him drying our glasses with the tails of his dirty shirt I insisted on hygiene, including that of clothes and hands. I was determined not to get rid of him. I would show that I was different from all those Western brides. Besides Maurice was fond of him. Sheikh Hussein had nursed him through recurrent bouts of malaria when they used to camp in tribal jungles. I did not complain to Maurice until Sheikh Hussein nearly got us expelled from the Club.

Mrs de Chazal, the wife of a Police Superintendent, had invited me to tea on the verandah of her spacious married quarters. We were chatting idly about this and that when, asking how much she tipped the sweeper each week, I said 'I give him five rupees, and you?' She told the Club Secretary. Sheikh Hussein had been quick to spot that, not being British, I was ignorant of Club rules. I had to tend a formal apology to the Club Committee, even though investigation revealed the sweeper had never received that money. Sheikh Hussein's salary was forty five rupees a month, an extra twenty had been worth the try. Maurice was furious.

'The man can be a rascal! I do not remember whether I have already told you what happened in West Khandesh when my Head Clerk warned me that he had heard a plaintiff offer Sheik Hussein a fifty rupee bribe to speak on his behalf. I had the bribe-giver paraded through the streets in hand-cuffs as a warning to others not to give bribes.'

'And Sheikh Hussein?'

'There was no proof that he had taken the money. He most certainly never spoke to me about the case. I felt he had been warned. Perhaps I should have been tougher, but there was no proof. As far as I was concerned he had done nothing wrong.'

After I noticed how the cost of a tonga ride to Connaught Circus was halved when, without haggling, it was I who paid the driver, I began to keep a strict watch over our finances. Every time Sheikh Hussein was sent to post a letter, he had to bring back a certificate of posting. Airmail stamps were expensive. When I was in America, a letter to Maurice cost as much as lunch in a cafeteria. I understood at last why, as their numbering showed, so many of Maurice's letters had not reached me and why his photograph had gone astray. As I whittled down his income, Sheikh Hussein became increasingly morose, hankering after the good old District days when, unbeknown to his master, opportunities abounded. At the end of three months he tried to enlist my help to restore his fortune. With the eloquence of conviction he explained how important Maurice had been in the District, how palatial our residence would be, how many servants we would have.

'In Khandesh Sahib had ten and me. Now, when we go back with ayah for Memsahib, make eleven and me!' With a grin of disgust he surveyed our cramped accommodation adding with a deep sigh. 'In District, Sahib very burrah Sahib, like King. In Delhi, Sahib only *Kalark,* pukka nobody.' He begged me to use my influence to persuade Maurice to get himself transferred back to a District.

A couple of weeks later Sheikh Hussein gave Maurice an ultimatum: 'Sahib must choose. Memsahib send back to Bilayat (England) or I go.' In the seven years he had been with Maurice he had amassed enough to retire into comfortable idleness. We subsequently discovered that whenever Maurice stayed with friends, Sheikh Hussein stole his master's petty cash knowing that if he noticed he would not tell his hosts that their servants were thieves. I was overjoyed the day Sheikh Hussein resigned. Abdul, his successor, was to become so much part of our family that I have written a book dedicated to him.*

I think it was on the third day after my arrival in Delhi that I met Masood.

We were sitting in front of our little verandah in the garden of the Club watching a tame mongoose weave in and out of a floral border and admiring the setting sun. Soon it would be time for evening bath and change into formal dress for dinner before walking the hundred yards to the main buildings. I had just finished a cigarette when Maurice said, 'By the way, Masood dropped in this afternoon to ask if I have any objection to his calling on you tomorrow around ten. He wants to see you alone. Remember, I used to write how he had improved my crusade against money-lenders in West-Khandesh. He is quite a chap old Masood. I know you will like him.'

*'Rishi' (Methuen, 1960)

One year Maurice's junior in the ICS Masood, an Oxford Boxing Blue, had succeeded Maurice in that remote tribal area, so cut off that touring had to be done on horseback. The inhabitants, the Bhils, were ruthlessly exploited by moneylenders. When a Bhil had to borrow money, to buy liquor or a bride, being illiterate he had to put a thumb-mark on a promissory note which grossly exaggerated his debt. And he was never given receipts for what he paid back. He was thus cheated thrice over because the interest was exorbitant, maybe 50%, and because the moneylender employed Pathan gangsters to collect at the end of their stick, a fourth criminal offence. When Bhils refused to pay moneylenders took them to the Civil Court where they were bound to lose. It was only the Bhil's confused, often unintelligible, word against the learned presentation of a lawyer hired by the usurer. The Judge, trained under British law, was biased in favour of the written document. English Contract Law advantages the cunning with lawyers and the small print, as some who have tried to get redress from an airline, or dry-cleaner or an insurance company know. Since tribal land could not be alienated, the Judge used to attach the crop, turning Bhils into moneylenders' slave labourers, working to pay a debt they could never fully discharge.

Maurice knew from experience that Bhils usually told the truth and decided cases accordingly in that part of his area where he was a Civil Judge. He would even ask the moneylender to show cause why he should not be prosecuted for perjury. He made clear to policemen and magistrates in the whole of his jurisdiction that Bhil complaints against moneylenders' cheating could not be ignored and should be treated as criminal complaints. But the moneylender and his thugs usually got off on Appeal. The Sessions Judge was a townsman, elevated from the Bar. He was ignorant of tribal conditions and found it impossible not to believe moneylenders whose books were impeccably kept, or the defence lawyers' cogent arguments.

Fortunately, going into Appeal was sufficiently expensive and time-consuming for moneylenders to realise that, so long as Maurice was there, it would not pay them to harrass Bhils, especially since Maurice used to hear their cases where it suited the Bhil, and not in the moneylender's town, so that the moneylender had to return after dark through panther infested jungle or spend an extra night away from home.

Masood, on taking over from Maurice, had gone one better. His method was as simple as it was ruthless. Whenever a Bhil complained that he had been cheated, Masood told the police to search thoroughly for the promissory note. If the moneylender produced it, he could be arrested and charged with cheating if the amount in the promissory note did not tally with what the Bhil said he had received. If the moneylender did not produce the note, the police searched his house, from roof-tiles to bedding-rolls and emptied everything into the streets, for the whole village to see. Since no IOU had been found, the Bhil could not be asked to pay; and the moneylender's loss of face was such that he left the village.

Masood's method was not orthodox, but nor was Masood; undoubtedly one of the most eccentric members of the ICS of our acquaintance.

I had been warned not to offer him alcohol or cigarettes. 'Alcohol and tobacco are taboo. Many Muslims drink and smoke, but Masood is a good Muslim. Quite a chap. You should get him to tell you how, with the help of his two brothers, he stopped a riot in his home town, just by walking arm in arm down the street, like a tank.'

'Like a tank' was so right. A tank with the neck of a bull and shoulders so broad that they filled the door as he pushed inside our drawing-room.

'May I come in? Maurice said you did not mind our being alone together.'

We shook hands. A painful experience. He sat down filling

the armchair, and dashed into speech like a child reciting a much rehearsed lesson. 'Maurice has spoken to me so often of your wisdom that I have made the journey specially to ask your advice. Please help me. I am in a terrible fix. I need the advice of a woman I can trust absolutely to keep what I am going to tell a secret. And there is nobody but you I can turn to'. I was flattered and intrigued. He kept wrenching the knuckles of his outsized hairy fingers, making them crackle.

'Whatever you tell me to do I will.'

Betrothed by his parents to a distant relative's daughter he had taken advantage of a chaperone's lax supervision to kiss his fiancée on several occasions. They were due to get married shortly. But, as Allah would have it, during a recent visit home he had fallen in love with a cousin and she with him. Could he call the arranged marriage off?

'Nobody will marry her now that she has been kissed!' he exclaimed piteously. I made certain that Masood did not use 'kissed' as a euphemism for something more compromising. I assured him the jilted girl would be the last person to broadcast an intimacy damaging to a reputation which would remain intact so long as he told no one, not even his beloved. Overjoyed, Masood almost crushed me in a fraternal embrace.

'Maurice was right. He did not exaggerate when he said you were wise! Bless you and may Allah give you a long life with many sons.'

Masood married his cousin. It had been rumoured that, during Partition he took an active part in the anti-Sikh riots of his jurisdiction. I saw him again, a few years later, in Lahore, where I had gone to report on General Ayub Khan's successful military coup. Masood's wife had recently died in childbirth. He had married her younger sister, a shy wisp of a girl 'to give the baby a mother.'

Although a Government official, he disapproved of military rule and introduced me to the Underground. He had become a strict vegetarian, and kept his head shaved in mourning for his wife. Over dinner, served by his second wife who did not sit at the table, he explained his method of keeping law and order in his last District.

That method was as novel as it was effective. However, I cannot imagine it being followed by anyone else. He would send word to those with grievances, particularly hot-heads and faction leaders, to meet him in the market place, and challenged them to a sit-down wrestling match. Facing his opponent, he would clasp his hand and bring it down on the table between them. Masood never lost. So great was his reputation for sheer strength that it always settled matters. He was not boasting. He was too straightforward for that. Eventually disillusioned with the government he resigned to devote himself to village uplift, turned Gandhian, wore handspun clothes and wrote a book about the simple life. The book had some success. He visited us once in London, during a cold wet winter. Practising what he preached he was bare-footed in open sandals, his powerful body loosely clad in a grey sacking sufficiently shapeless not to be pronounced trousers. From his huge shoulders hung a garment, neither jacket nor shirt, and he was draped in a shawl of coarse camel wool. The width of his bulk thus enlarged, he looked like a bald Roman Senator. On a lecture tour sponsored by the publisher, he was on his way to extol the merits of celibacy and the simple life to rich American widows.

I had not been in Delhi for a fortnight when I was summoned to the phone.

'I am Shungloo' said a voice. 'Mister Morris asked me to bring it. Can you arrange for two men to help unload. I am sending it over in an hour if convenient.'

Shungloo. Probably Chinese like Fu Manchoo. What was so heavy it needed two men to unload? Maurice had not mentioned anything.

An hour later a large limousine pulled up by the tiny verandah of our quarters. A liveried chauffeur opened the boot, with the help of the sweeper and the gardener's assistant, organised by Sheikh Hussein, heaved out a large slab of polished sandstone the colour of anaemic carrots with a bas-relief showing a large warrior astride a small horse framed between the facing bills of two large pelicans each one squatting on a lotus bud atop a column. The warrior's long sword, dangling beneath the horse's hooves threatened to catch the stirrup, and the enormity of his turban, dwarfing rider and steed, would, in real life, topple both. 'It' weighed, we subsequently discovered, three hundredweight.

'Good God!' Maurice exclaimed! 'Darling, I thought I was getting you a statuette for the mantelpiece as a wedding present.' Shortly before leaving India to get married Maurice had been to Jaisolmer, a Princely State on the edge of the desert. Charmed by the carvings in the old town he had been taken to the workshops where tradition was still kept alive. After admiring the memorial slab for a deceased Rajput, he had ordered a small replica of horse and rider. 'Well, never mind, Darling, it will come in handy one day and there's lots of room for loving inscriptions.' Being superstitious, I refused to have the tombstone inside our quarter. It kept guard in front of the porch and followed us whenever we moved - Maurice having become inordinately attached to it. Eventually, it cost me two pounds for removers to lose it when taking our things from a bedsit in Brondesbury to a flat in Earl's Court.

Maurice had no luck with his presents. When he applied to the Reserve Bank of India to send me money for an engagement ring I bought him five silk ties and matching pochettes with the sanctioned fifty dollars.

And the saga of my engagement present does credit to the combined bureaucratic inventiveness of the American and the British Customs. Two days before I was due to leave New York I received a Customs notification that an ivory cigarette box had arrived. Besides paying a hefty amount in duty since it was not an 'antique', that is not over a hundred years old, I had to be present at the opening of the parcel because the packaging had to be vetted by a censor in case it carried subversive propaganda. This vetting had been a real curse on our arrival in the United States. We had been forced to spend ten days in Jacksonville, Florida, while censors, and translators, waded through mounds of old newsprint in which our belongings had been wrapped. In vain had we assured them they could destroy the lot. No. Crumpled bits of *Paris Soir* had to be pulled out of shoes, flattened out, and vetted. 'Don't you know there's a war going on?' had been officialdom's explanation. Alas, the war was still on. Naturally, I instructed the Customs to send the package to my London address.

The package arrived in London months after I did. The postman brought a Customs form requiring me to appear in person or to send an authorised representative at HM's Customs Office to witness the opening of the parcel, which, since the invoice specified that there was kapok in the wrapping, had to be fumigated. I was reminded of the French Deputy who had stated in the Chamber that one must never forget that 'L'Angleterre est une île qui a la particularité toute particulière d'être entourée d'eau de tous côtés.' As, by then, I had been given a passage to Bombay, I instructed the Customs to send my parcel back to India. I do not remember exactly how long it took my engagement present to arrive. All I know is that by the time Maurice retrieved it our son had been born. Nearly two years had gone by since he sent me that box and he had to pay a hefty amount in demurrage, The box is lovely. Exquisitely carved. However, as it is entirely fretted it cannot be used to store cigarettes. Since it is not lined, it is also unsuitable for jewels. I keep it under glass in our drawing-room.

8

Delhi that was

Life in the ICS was formal. Even when he was living in tents, touring the District, Maurice changed before dinner, like a Somerset Maugham character, though sometimes only into pyjamas.

'What for? You were alone.'

'Darling, you don't understand. Before dinner one always had a bath, in a tin-tub and smelling of the kerosene to heat the water, but a bath. One was so sticky, sweaty and dusty. A bath was essential. Afterwards, naturally, one put on clean clothes. A dinner jacket, somehow, helps to keep up morale. It is so easy to let oneself go if one does not keep up appearances. One shaves every morning, so one dresses every evening.'

Sheikh Hussein used to dress my husband, until I put a stop to it. To watch him putting Maurice's socks on was more than I could bear.

Dressing up was why, when I wrote from America asking what kind of clothes I should bring, evening gowns had been so high on Maurice's list. Taking advantage of the fact that long dresses were in scant demand because of the war, I bought many in the Christmas sales.

'Are you an entertainer?' the sales lady at Marshall Fields asked packing ten gowns. Extravagant as it may seem, I did not spend a fortune. The best three cost fifty dollars each, the rest were practically given away. For a mere five hundred dollars I must have been one of the best dressed European women in Delhi with forty new evening-gowns. A year later, motherhood having altered my shape, they delighted those who bought the ones I could not get into.

Life in Delhi was not only formal, it was extremely hierarchical. Protocol, as Maurice explained, laid down precedence with such rigidity that who sat next to whom at dinner could, sometimes, assume an importance so disproportionate that many a feminine feud was sparked off by what had been, perhaps wrongly, construed as a deliberate insult. When we entertained in the club dining-room, Maurice supervised the seating.

It was not just protocol I had to adapt to, but the British. Maurice had invited the Hydaris, their two daughters, the Symons and Sen Gupta, his own boss. I sat at one end of the table, Sir Akbar Hydari on my right, Sen Gupta on my left. Pregnancy did not agree with me. Teeth clenched against the smell of the food, I could not utter a word and had to rush out to be sick. Obliged to change, I came back in time for the second course. Like a fool, instead of staying in our quarters, I kept rushing off, being sick, coming back. Dinner went on as if I did not leave the table, despite the fact that, having messed up my gowns, I had to change three times. Nobody asked how I felt. Had this happened in America or France somebody, preferably a woman, would have shown concern for my ordeal, accompanied me to bed and insisted I stay there.

The next day, Sen Gupta was waiting in Maurice's office.

'Zinkin, you look tired. Overwork, I suppose. I have decided to send you to Simla for three months, the air will do you good.' Maurice was too junior to recess in Simla. Sen Gupta was making an exception because the Delhi heat was not agreeing with my condition.

'Calling', the dropping of visiting cards by senior service wives on new arrivals, epitomised for me the extent to which Delhi society, entirely official, unlike Bombay's, was starched in formality. After a card had been 'dropped', usually by a servant, one was expected to call, fairly soon, preferably at the time indicated in the bottom corner. In due course one was invited for lunch at the week-end or for dinner. Needless to say, dinner was always black tie, uniform, long skirt.

Those dinners! . . . How different from everything I had been used to. The fingerbowls adorned with floating rose petals were for one's mouth, not one's fingers. In France only the mouths of small children could be washed at the table. The first time sardines on toast followed a chocolate meringue cake swathed in Chantilly I thought there had been a mistake, but Maurice later explained that dessert must be followed by a savoury. What gastronomical barbarism! And nothing in France, or America, had prepared me for sex segregation at the end of meals, nor for the blatant way in which 'the gentlemen were invited to water the garden' while the hostess asked if one wanted to go to the bathroom. In France such matters were never mentioned. Guests were expected to have dealt with their needs before going out.

Maurice was much amused when I told him how I had wept because a young man I was infatuated with had asked for the WC.

'But, Darling, be reasonable! He obviously had a need.'

'He should have controlled it or left.'

'Perhaps he did not want to leave: enjoyed your company too much. How long had he been with you?' Claude had come for lunch. Only when I enquired, after tea, whether he would like to stay for dinner did he reveal the earthier side of his nature. 'Poor boy! he must have been bursting!'

'But *I* did not go to the loo.'

'Women have bigger bladders; besides there is nothing shameful about nature's calls. Your attitude, if I may be permitted to say so, is ridiculous.'

I found the Club atmosphere stifling. So formal. So many

areas - like the reading room - out of bounds to women. Not enough Indian members. Indians came to play tennis, eat, drink, perhaps swim and dance, but with the very conspicuous exception of Keith Roy, there were no Indian residents. Challenged, Maurice explained that, unlike the Royal Bombay Yacht Club where Indians could only come as guests, in Delhi there was no restriction but that children were not allowed to stay at the Club.

'Indians marry young, so by the time they are senior enough to afford to stay at the Club, they have children.'

Children were debarred from staying at the Club but could use some of its facilities, particularly the swimming pool, the tennis courts and the extensive gardens with the terraces where copious teas - watercress, cucumber and tomato sandwiches, buns, toast with strawberry jam and fruit cakes - were served under flowery arbours. Eating out was not without hazards from celestial predators. Dive-bombing crows would snatch a piece of cake midway between plate and lips. The moment one got distracted some impudent chipmunk, that enchanting squirrel elegantly striped with the marks on its back by Rama's caressing fingers, would pounce to partake of one's treat. Scampering back to safety the tiny thief would remain within view, munching loot daintily held between tiny hands, head cocked to one side, tail questioning the air, ready to dash down for seconds.

The residents were service bachelors or grass widowers with wives in the UK with the children or in a few cases couples like ourselves, on the waiting list for permanent accommodation. A few of the quarters were reserved for up-country members. Apart from the ICS there were some Indian Policemen (Members of the All India Police Service) and some wartime experts. The Armed Forces used the Club extensively but had their own hostels.

Club residents knew each other. They all worked for the Government of India, often in the same department. They breakfasted and dined in the same room - often, if they were single, at the same table. Moreover they kept bumping into each other at the swimming pool. Yet the extent to which they kept to themselves staggered me.

I still remember with dismay the case of John Shattuck. We had dined together a couple of times and sipped whisky in our little drawing room. His quarters faced ours across the wide alley leading to the main buildings.

'Have you been away?' I had not seen him for the best part of the two weeks he had been bed-ridden, tended by his bearer. Had I known I would have brought him books, kept him company.

'I was afraid to impose,' he blushed when I reproved him. British reticence shocks me even now. Fear of imposing, fear of getting involved - or is it fear of being under an obligation? - is a British disease.

The only exception was Nemenyi who lived two verandahs away. But Nemenyi was not British. Our friendship began in a most ridiculous manner. Maurice owned half a horse. Every morning, before breakfast, Jane was brought for a couple of hours, her other rider rode in the evenings. As soon as my riding breeches were ready, I began to ride. I loved those morning outings in the brisk dry cold of the Delhi winter. Until the sun had been at work it was so cold I used to set off with fur mittens, a woollen scarf, a pullover and a jacket. Jane's groom ran behind us to gather what I discarded as the temperature rose, by some thirty degrees fahrenheit within a quarter of an hour.

I was galloping along Kingsway, enjoying the smell of dew on the grass, when at considerable risk to himself, a madman grabbed Jane's bit, stopping her dead in her tracks. I nearly fell off.

'Young lady, I have saved your life! Permit me to introduce myself. My name is Nemenyi. If I am not mistaken, you must be Zinkin's new wife. It is indeed lucky that I decided to come this way for my morning walk. Usually I go towards the racecourse. Heaven only knows what could have happened. This is a very tall and powerful horse. You might have been killed. Permit me to help you dismount. I shall walk her back to the Club. A runaway horse needs time to cool down.'

'Jane is not runaway! You gave me a fright! Let me go on with my ride; please take our hands off.' I galloped away and, just to prove I was in control, dashed round King George's statue three times before galloping past my would-be saviour.

At dinner that evening Nemenyi invited himself to our table. Tall, grey-haired, green-eyed, middle-aged and gallant, Nemenyi, 'Phipps' to his friends, was Hungarian. An ex-cavalry officer who prided himself on his horsemanship.

'Back in Budapest I used to ride bare-back, without stirrups. Haute Ecole. One had to pick up a handkerchief at full gallop. I am terribly sorry if I scared you. But you looked out of control . . . reins flapping, toes down . . .' Not having learnt to ride I had committed all the don'ts but, as Phipps conceded after giving me my first lesson, I had a natural seat.

Phipps had two strings to his bow. He never tired of telling you how good he was at both. The oddity is that he really was good, and everybody knew it. Horsemanship was one string. Whenever one of the horses of the Viceroy's Guard became fractious, it was left to Phipps to break it back in. Finance was his other string. He was one of the wartime experts in Maurice's ministry.

The only other thing of which Phipps boasted was being married to a Professor Stella Kramrisch, who lived in Calcutta and taught Art History at the University. Out and out continental, I felt much more at home with Phipps than with the other residents of the Club.

I do not remember whether it was Phipps who introduced me to Fori, a fellow Hungarian, married to B K Nehru - Biju to everybody. Biju, a cousin of Pandit Nehru was senior to Maurice in the ICS and later became one of India's leading diplomats. Fori was inseparable from Kitty Shiva Rao.

Kitty had married Premy Wagle's uncle. Lady Rama Rao had already told me in Bombay that Kitty and I had much in common despite the fact that Kitty was much older.

'She is a darling. You will simply love her. We all do.' Lady Rama Rao had explained that Kitty's marriage was most unusual, arranged by Annie Besant the Theosophist, in an attempt to prove that a meeting of minds is all that is required for marriages to succeed. Shiva Rao, a Hindu, and Kitty, an Austrian Jewess, were her disciples.

In those early days, when I found everything so new, their company provided me with a welcome refuge from the boring company of wives whose conversation revolved around the state of their infants' bowels, the progress of their potted plants, and their servants' misdeeds - more or less in that order. Few had a university education, though they knew the Latin names of plants, and some had a dab of veneer from finishing school. Many took no interest in the country where they had to spend the best part of their lives and knew little of its ancient civilisation. Most of them nostalgically strove, against heavy odds, and often with surprising success to recreate the Surbitons or the Somersets of their roots, complete with tinned kippers, steak and kidney pudding and Irish stew, beautiful gardens and well-run houses. India only impinged upon them through prickly heat and a well-founded dread of dysentery. Everything raw had to be soaked in 'pinky', a solution of potassium permanganate believed to kill the dreaded bacillus. They vied with each other in their obsessive obsession to control servants. Many times I was warned by a well-meaning hostess to keep all the groceries under lock and key, to dole out each morning the day's ration measured by the spoonful. For servants, one cigarette-tinful of rice or cereal and three teaspoonfuls of tea and one of sugar per person. For the masters, too, tea and sugar, had to be spooned out every day.

'My dear, unless you keep a strict watch, they will eat you

out of house and home! They even smuggle rice and sugar to feed their families! The cooks are proper thieves. You *must* check each item they bring from the bazaar, and make sure they don't overcharge you. The best way is to compare prices with those of other cooks. And even then, all cooks charge more, but that is their perk.'

In the fifteen years we stayed in India I locked nothing and doled nothing out. The only time I kept a strict watch was with Sheikh Hussein. Of course I did, from time to time, cut back the cook's bill when it was excessive. Maybe our servants drank their tea too strong and too sweet, so what? measuring spoonfuls, except for recipes, was, I thought, indecent when a bottle of whisky cost exactly what our bearer earned a month.* However, that did not seem to bother women sentenced to a domestic idleness they tried to expiate by measuring tea-dust. To expect such women to take an interest in politics would have been daft. Even the Irish and Scottish wives, who were usually graduates, and took an intelligent interest in India, did not find politics exciting, perhaps because their husbands were so absorbed by talking of the day to day problems of administration that politics as such remained in the background.

Yet, at the end of 1945 Indian politics were fascinating. With the end of the war, independence was clearly coming. The question was not if, but when and how. Above all, would power be handed over to one State of Undivided India as Kitty and Fori fervently hoped, or to two States of India and Pakistan as Jinnah demanded, or to three states of India, Pakistan and Bengal, or to four states of India, Pakistan, Bengal

*We paid our servants more than Indians did, yet when we left India in 1960 that equation still held good. I believe this was still the case a quarter of a century later. It is a sign of India's poverty that a respected skilled worker, as the bearer is, usually with a family to keep, earns a bottle of whisky per month plus his lodging, uniform, tea, sugar, cereals but nothing for the rest of his family and has neither holidays nor time off even at weekends.

and Princely India? My political education began in the company of my new-found friends. Maurice was among the Civil Servants in Delhi who favoured Independence with Dominion Status, preferably for one India.

There were redeeming exceptions among Delhi's memsahibs. Lady Tymms stands out to this day. One of Maurice's jobs was to provide financial advice for her husband, who was in charge of Civil Aviation and was later to become Director General of ICAO. Soon his wife invited us to dinner.

'Call me Millie; everyone does.' Pretty in black velvet, kittenish despite her age and silvery hair, Millie sported the broad Cockney of her chorus girl beginnings with charming grace. Wonderfully warm and lively, loveable, unaffected, she was a real gem.

There were in Delhi large military contingents waiting to be repatriated. The officers, who were Club guests as a matter of course, were also welcome in private homes. In the absence of a resident British middle, or working class, the troops had nowhere to relax. Lady Tymms ran a Social club for them. After dinner, every Saturday evening, an army truck collected me and other volunteers to dance with the Tommies. Millie had warned me not to wear open-toed sandals or good evening-gowns. Dancing with young men in knobbled boots and a surfeit of energy is an act of kindness requiring dedication. I used to get back with blood-stained shoes and a torn skirt. We adopted a private and a corporal. they came in turn to spend their day off at the Club. To avoid embarrassment in the stately dining-room under the critical glare of the servants who were unduly snobbish, we used to picnic in the garden, or by the swimming pool.

'Tonight we will eat in our room. Tell the Head Bearer in the dining-room. We shall be three. As it is Friday, there's bound to be fish. No meat. We have a Hindu guest,' Maurice said before going to his office and said something in Marathi to Sheikh Hussein.

Our drawing-room was very small. By the time things had been organised for dinner it looked over-crowded with a table in the middle, flanked by the sofa and two armchairs with nests of small tables near at hand laden with bowls of peanuts, cashew nuts and potato crisps, ash-trays and coasters for glasses. On a side table, borrowed from the bedroom, Sheikh Hussein had arranged an ice bucket, soda bottles, angostura bitters, lemon slices and our ration of spirits. As there was an acute shortage of gin and whisky, Phipsons, the drinks retailers, operated an unofficial but rigid rationing system allowing established customers one bottle of each a month. Anybody wanting more had to go to the black-market or have a friend in the armed forces where spirits were not rationed and only cost nine rupees instead of forty five.

To my astonishment, as soon as Maurice got home, he gave Sheikh Hussein the evening off.

'Our guest wants to remain incognito.'

'Why?'

'He is a senior Congressman from Bengal. You may remember that Gandhi asked his followers not to fraternise with the rulers and to boycott us. Our guest does not want to be seen in our company.'

K C Neogy, later Minister for Commerce, arrived shortly after dark. He was the first Congressman I met. I remember him not so much because he was the first, or because he was exquisitely courteous in an old-fashioned way, or because he was gentle and cultured and wore a sparkling white handspun ajkhan, but because he kept popping in and out of sight in a manner most unbefitting a man old enough to be my father. Each time a waiter knocked at the door KC Neogy fled to our bedroom. Caught short, when coffee arrived he ducked behind the sofa.

Maurice had made many Indian friends at Cambridge.

It was Manzur Qadir, later Foreign Minister of Pakistan,

who had first given him the idea of going into the ICS. Another was Maharaj Nagendra Singh, later to become Chief Justice of the International Court, who joined the service the same year as Maurice.

'Nagu' was the younger brother of the Maharajah of Dungarpur, the most distinguished house in India, descendants of the sun, of the same ancestry as the Maharanas of Udaipur, but of the elder line. They shared with Udaipur the distinction of never having given a daughter in marriage to a Moghul Emperor.

I met Nagu during my first Delhi winter. Over dinner I mentioned that, beside teaching French and doing research at the University of Wisconsin, I had washed dishes and waited in a cafeteria. Horror flicked through Nagu's cheerful face . . . I could almost read his thoughts. Amused, I assured him that in the US such versatility was normal, especially in academe where many of the best people worked their way through college. To clinch my point, I added it was normal for the children of VIPs to earn pocket-money washing cars, clearing snow and dead leaves, harvesting fruit, running errands.

'In France or England it's not done but the Americans are right. It teaches the dignity of labour and is at the core of democracy.'

'Maybe. But Taya, please don't keep talking about it. You might be misunderstood. Ours is a very orthodox society, lots of taboos . . . only Untouchables sweep.'

After coffee he asked me to do him a favour. He had come to Delhi to inspect a potential bride-groom for a niece. The boy was a student at St Stephen's College. Right family, matching horoscopes. Could I accompany him to see if the boy would make a good husband?

'Why don't you take your niece and let her decide?'

'My dear Taya,' Nagu laughed at my ignorance, 'you forget we are pukka Rajputs. Our women are in purdah. Do you know the only time Mother has crossed the threshold of our

Palace was as a bride, carried in her dholi - a litter - with the curtains drawn shut? She has never left the zenana, not even once. When Maurice came to stay he did not meet her. My niece will set eyes on her husband for the first time during the wedding ceremony. She will of course have seen photographs. That is why I would like your opinion.' Nagu's mother crossed the threshold for the second time after her death, to be cremated. Only then did Nagu take his wife out of purdah.

We drove to St Stephen's College to view the candidate. He did not expect us. A handsome lad, airforce moustache, well spoken, a trifle shy. His room was tidy. Nagu left us alone for a while so that I might ask questions only an inquisitive foreigner could be permitted. He did not believe in purdah, wanted to work as an engineer, hoped to marry a girl with enough education to share his life. He sat on the edge of his bed, dangling feet in tennis shoes, as we chatted. He was fond of tennis and cricket. He did not want a large family - three children at most. He smoked his pipe, with my permission, and said he did not approve of the Rajput dedication to whisky. A relative 'drank like a fish' and that had put him off liquor. My tentative verdict was favourable.

'Arranging marriages is such a tremendous responsibility; especially with us Hindus. There is no divorce. Go-betweens cannot be trusted, sometimes they are bribed; and parents make mistakes. That is why I wanted a woman's opinion. One cannot be too careful.'

Nagu was so right. The sister of one of Maurice's friends had been married to a handsome and wealthy nawab. Nobody warned her father that he was a drunk and a lecher. After a traumatic honeymoon his bride ran away to her parents - a visit after the honeymoon was customary - and did not go back. Her husband was eventually hanged for drowning a prostitute in his bath tub.

'I cannot wait for you to meet Manzur. Of all my friends

he was my mother's favourite.' We were on our way to Lahore where I had to enrol to finish my studies as Delhi's Medical School came under the University of the Punjab with headquarters in Lahore.

Manzur was waiting for us at the station. I cannot remember why he could not put us up. In India one never stayed in hotels, always with friends, or with friends of friends. Hotels were for foreigners, outsiders and businessmen. Manzur drove us straight from the station to Khushwant Singh, one of his closest friends, who proved a willing host. Small world, Khushwant had spent time in Paris before the war and we had friends in common. Indeed, before I left to join Maurice in India, I had been told to look Khushwant up: 'His father was knighted by the Viceroy, so he must be persona grata with the powers that be and he is *most* amusing.'

Manzur and Khushwant were different as chalk and cheese. Khushwant's extrovert machismo has obliterated my first recollections of Manzur whose quiet restraint was, over the years, to make a profound impression of intergrity, courage and cultured wisdom.

When I first met Khushwant he was ebulliently in revolt against tradition. Very much to the Left, the only reason he gave for wearing a turban over his long hair knotted at the top in a bun and growing a beard which he clipped - was the effect discarding those outward signs of Sikhism would have on his father.

Manzur and Khushwant were inseparable, so were their wives. Kawal was beautifully Junoesque with large brown eyes and a thick plait of hair. Both women painted; Azgadi, Manzur's wife, took painting sufficiently seriously to spend time in the residential academy of Roerich, a White Russian painter of note. Khushwant helped me through the labyrinthine maze of the academic red-tape created to deter applicants who, like myself, did not belong to the run of the mill.

Lahore, with few journalists, no foreign correspondents or

industrialists, was more provincial than Bombay, less formal and cosmopolitan than Delhi. In 1945 Lahore was cultured and homogeneous, a shining example of harmony between Muslims, Hindus, Sikhs and Christians. Thanks to the Hindu, Sikh and Christian example, Muslim girls were not in strict purdah; many of them went to college and a girl with books strapped to the back of her bicycle was not an unusual sight. In the splendid Lawrence Gardens students went for walks in mixed groups. In Delhi sex segregation was the norm, much as I had observed in pre-Civil War Spain.

One evening at the club I asked Khushwant why the pleats of the sari of one of the ladies on the dance floor did not flow down from the waist but fanned out from below her hips.

'Sheila is a Christian, so she winds her sari round twice.' And he added that Lahore Christians were very different from the Christians of South India, the 'bread Christians,' ex-Untouchables. In Lahore they came from good families and had been converted out of conviction.

Khushwant's time in Paris had not been wasted. He waltzed well. Suddenly I became aware that something undefinable was wrong. The Club membership was mixed. Indian couples and European couples were on the floor. But we were the only mixed couple and I could feel silent reproof in the way older Europeans were glaring at me. In Bombay or Delhi such racism was unthinkable. Membership of the Royal Bombay Yacht Club was restricted to Europeans, but Indian guests mixed freely and the Willingdon, which had a swimming pool was mixed.

Shortly after our visit to Lahore Khushwant invited us to his brother's wedding in Delhi, the only Sikh wedding to which I have been. I remember the incongruous sight of a bearded face hidden under a tinsel fringe, the delicious food and Lady Sobha Singh, Kushwant's mother, a charming old lady devoid of pretensions, kind enough to encourage my faltering Urdu.

It was shortly after that wedding that I met the Viceroy. Walking to the reception in our afternoon best, Maurice warned me to speak only in answer to questions. The result was disastrous. It was a very official do. The Viceroy did not mingle with his guests. Instead an ADC would usher the chosen few, one by one, into the august presence seated at a small table in a recess, mention the newcomer's name and help with sitting down. An impressive majordomo in imperial regalia brought a fresh pot of tea and wafer-thin cucumber and water-cress sandwiches and a plate of pastry. How many cups of tea did the Viceroy drink? Or did he simply pretend to keep one company? He looked sad, tired, manfully grey. The majordomo poured my tea, passed the sugar, the milk, the eats. Waiting for the conversation to start I nibbled a sandwich, then another, then a small meringue topped with chantilly. Was my host lost in deep thoughts? Had he seen me? I drank the tea, and put the cup back on the saucer with a small clatter. In a desperate effort to make me feel at ease, Lord Wavell asked:

'Have you been to Simla?'

'No, your Excellency.'

'In Simla, there are violets in Spring.'

There was nothing I could say. I finished the meringue in silence and was taken back to the main room by a second ADC while the first brought another guest to the viceregal table. Our ordeal, Lord Wavell's and mine, had lasted an excruciating twelve minutes.

Formality in India was not confined to the Viceroy and the ICS world. The lower the social scale the stricter the do's and don'ts. Adherence to rules used to be ruthlessly enforced.

Thus Lady Hydari, the Swedish wife of the Member for Commerce and Industry, used to complain that servants whose jobs were on the ground-floor refused, with the exception of the bearer, to work on the first floor. 'That's why we have such a large staff. Even more pay doesn't tempt them. Ridiculous, but that's how it is!' Grooms did not cut grass for horses so we had two servants for Jane. When Maurice was a bachelor, camping in tents in the districts, he had eleven servants, including messengers, to look after him. The cook cooked, somebody else washed up, usually a couple of plates three times a day. Even in 1960, drivers did not wash cars, and our driver went to the barber for his daily shave. Bearers did not dust, second boys did not sweep. Job demarcation is less rigid now, but when I first came to India it was cast in steel.

Rigidity worked both ways. When Mildred, my American friend, was looking for a bearer, I asked Abdul to recommend somebody. We were having coffee at Mildred's when a bearer sent by Abdul arrived. Mildred asked him to sit down. The man fled. Abdul, who did not know I had been present, was indignant.

'Memsahib, you have blackened my face! Nobody can work for that 'pagli' - mad woman - she is dangerously mad. Isaac had never been so insulted by a memsahib in his life, and he has been in service for many years. The way he was treated!' All my poor friend had done was to behave in Delhi as she would have done in New York. She did not know that for a servant to sit in the presence of his employer constitutes unpardonable impertinence. Once when I was travelling alone and not feeling well I asked Abdul to stay in my compartment. He would not sit down and for the thirty hours between Delhi and Bombay, insisted on standing or squatting on his heels.

9

Memsahib malgré moi

On arrival in Delhi I applied to enrol at Medical School. Had I stayed in America a little longer I would have left with a PhD in Biochemistry and a Doctorate in Medicine. When I wrote to Maurice suggesting we postpone our marriage by a year so that I might get my degrees he answered: 'There is no reason why you should not finish Medical School here, or so I gathered from Ackroyd, the Director of the Pasteur Institute. But I think that recognition of your French credits would be a matter for special consideration. However, an ICS wife has privileges.'

And again a few days later, 'I spoke to Gwyer, the Vice-Chancellor of Delhi University about whether they would accept your French qualifications and he thought it would be all right.' In America my French qualifications had been accepted outright. It never crossed my mind, especially after Maurice's letters, that in India things might be different.

My application was rejected on the ground that I did not have a Punjab Matriculation! Sir Maurice Gwyer had left India, there was nobody I could turn to for help. Getting that Matriculation involved, amongst other things, writing an essay in Urdu. I took Urdu lessons three times a week while protesting to the University that the French Baccalauréat, one year of pre-Med and four years of Medicine at the Sorbonne, not to mention three years of post-graduate research in Wisconsin, ought to exempt me from the Punjab Matric.

After six months of correspondence they waived the Matric and I was asked to apply for admission to Medical School between two dates mentioned on the enclosed form. This I did. By return of post I was informed that I had missed the last date for applying by a whole month and would have to apply again at the onset of the next academic year.

I applied, a year later, and was accepted as a full-time boarder at the Lady Hardinge Medical School - a residential college for Indian girls. The rules of residence were very strict. I would be allowed out twice a week till ten pm. By then we had a son. Not having parents in India with whom I could leave our baby I applied for special dispensation to live out. There was such a lot of anti-British feeling that I was told that to make an exception for an ICS wife, particularly a non-Indian ICS wife, was out of the question.

When I was six years old, I had been called upon, by circumstance, to help in an emergency blood-letting. Watching the relief it gave my beloved grand-mother I decided, there and then, that I would become a doctor like my father. Fired by a genuine sense of vocation I continued to study medicine despite the war and the exodus, first in Toulouse, then in Haiti. Once in America, to bypass the quota for admission to Medical School, I slogged at para-medical research in biochemistry, a science which did not thrill me. And now, because of politics, I was licked.

It is a miracle that anger and frustration did not destroy our marriage, especially since Maurice did not appear to appreciate the extent of my devastation. Nothing was turning out as expected. Instead of the house to which we were entitled, with dining-room, drawing-room, verandahs, two or three bedrooms with dressing-rooms and bathrooms, kitchen, scullery, servants' quarters and half an acre of garden, we were living in one hostel room, with a baby. Half a horse costing as much as a baby, we had been forced to give up riding. Maurice's salary which would, before the war, have been more than ample, had been eroded by inflation of over 300% so that, despite a 17½% marriage allowance, we were almost poor. Board and lodging, the bearer, the baby's ayah, his powdered milk, and our ration of spirits, absorbed what Maurice earned, leaving me with seventy-five rupees a month for everything else:- cigarettes, Urdu lessons, soft drinks, stamps, entertaining and clothes. It was a curious existence teetering between luxury and poverty. I sold some of my jewelry. To save on tongas we cycled in dinner jacket and evening-gown. We had no margin.

Soon after it became clear that I would have to wait to get into Medical School I applied for a job in the Ministry of Information and Broadcasting. The job had been suggested by Mrs Laxshmanan, the French wife of a senior Indian in that Ministry. It was a good and interesting job, paying 1,500 rupees a month, a job for which I was eminently qualified.

The post had to be sanctioned by Finance. Information and Broadcasting, like Roads, Ports and Airports, came under Communications and it was Maurice, as Deputy Financial Adviser Communications, who had to sanction it. He turned it down, reducing me to giving French lessons for pin-money. It was years before I realised he had been right. The mood in India was so anti-British that he would have been accused of nepotism. More serious, he would have been expected to show favour to an organisation swollen with temporary appointments regularly due for review.

How Prem Singh became my Urdu teacher I have forgotten. I expect one of Maurice's clerks must have recommended him. Tall, lanky, slim, narrow-wristed like a woman, Prem Singh was good looking by Indian standards, being very fair, with amber skin and blue-black hair, 'like a raven's wing' he once remarked complacently. His fingers, greasy from frequent contact with his generously oiled mop smudged everything. To protect my cigarettes from the rancid taste of coconut oil I used to set aside the cigarettes intended for him. Prem Singh's coquetry extended to the length of his fingernails. The little finger of his right hand used to fascinate me. Why should anybody grow a nail an inch long? To scoop wax out of ears? As a status symbol?

Three times a week, immaculate in white trousers and a cricketer's sweater, he taught me from a varnacular primer. Helping himself to a State Express 555 cigarette without waiting to be offered, he would quiz me, prefacing each question with 'Mind, don't cheat! Don't look at the book. How do you say, "The cow is my mother?"' His English was surprisingly good for such a lousy teacher. We parted company very soon, but not before he took us to see his native village.

Maurice who had accepted the invitation because he thought it would be an interesting experience for me, gave me a thorough briefing on how to behave. I was not to shake hands, but stick to the *Namascar*, the Indian greeting with folded hands. Contact with the Untouchables we were, would pollute Caste Hindus.

'In towns they are not very particular, but in villages these taboos are very strong. Did I tell you what happened in West Khandesh when I was Assistant Collector? Well listen, and take note. It will help you to avoid making the same faux-pas. I was on tour not far from headquarters when one of the leading pleaders took me to see the temple in the village where I was camping that night. Had I been in India longer I would not have gone. I visited the temple and gave the God the customary rupee. Next morning in the local newspaper, there was an editorial about the desecration of that temple. Should the temple be handed over to Untouchables, or had it been so irretrievably polluted by my visit that it ought to be condemned?'

Maurice also warned me that it is considered very rude not to eat or drink what is being offered.

'Once when I was on tour during a cholera epidemic to make sure the villagers got inoculated against the disease, in village after village I was offered milk. It had not been boiled, the glass was never clean, sometimes a fly or ant might be floating in it, but had I refused, the villagers would have been so offended that I could not have persuaded them to get inoculated. And, Darling, leaving food is considered an insult to one's host. We shall have to eat everything we are given. As you may have noticed, spicy food does not agree with me. Fortunately you like curry. So, between us, we should be all right.' I loved the Club's Sunday curries with their assortments of chutneys and pickles just as much as Maurice liked semolina, rice and tapioca puddings.

Prem Singh called for us in a bright-red open two-seater car. There was ample room in the boot for me, and he had put cushions in it.

'I hope you will be comfortable', he said, helping me to climb in. 'My friend's car is honoured by your presence Djinkin Sahib,' he added, holding the door open for Maurice to sit in front. Prem Singh, like many Indians, could not pronounce Z at the beginning of a word.

We set off in the explosive salvo from a petulant exhaust. It was a fine Sunday morning. The air was brittle with sunshine; the sky, untrammelled except by the flight of birds. Punctured here and there by the Majesty of Moghul remains, the monotonous plain lay flat, denuded after harvest. Monochrome villages dotted empty fields, Persian wheels stood still. Crocodiles of peasants and humped cattle with flapping dewlap crawled, leaving trails of fine dust, suspended in mid-air, in defiance of gravity. Not a cloud, not a breeze. Timelessness hung over the countryside to the creaking of the huge wooden wheels of bullock-carts. As we reached our destination Maurice observed for my benefit that Prem Singh's was a typical Jat village: Clusters of flat-roofed adobe houses with scant apertures, narrow winding alleys with open sewers, adobe-coloured mangy pie-dogs and stray cattle wistfully chewing cud. Dark cow-dung cakes imprinted by hand, drying on walls. Dust and flies eveywhere. Alerted by the car's exhaust, the entire village rushed forth, submerging us. Two welcoming garlands of marigold and tinsel were ceremoniously hung round our necks by the headman, who shepherded us into a house, saving us from the milling crowd. The headman was Prem Singh's father. To my surprise he spoke no English. When I visited Senegal before the war, village headmen in places far more distant from Dakar than this village was from Delhi spoke some French. French colonisation had, I whispered to Maurice, been more efficient. Prem Singh translated the paternal welcome address and Maurice's reply. Fluent in Marathi Maurice spoke no Urdu. Prem Singh translated so loudly that even the deaf could here. It dawned on me that the purpose of inviting us to his village was to enhance, by Maurice's presence, his own and his family's prestige, not - as I had naively imagined - to show me the village. The house engulfing us consisted of two rooms seperated from each other by a patio. It was oddly bare, as if emptied of its contents for the occasion.

'Please, Your Honour, sit. Food is being brought. We hope it is to your liking.' In the furthest room a sheet had been spread over a trestle table, flanked by two dusty chairs. Everybody, who could, squeezed into the doorway to watch us eat, obstructing light and air.

'Are they not going to eat with us?' I whispered. Maurice said that honoured guests eat alone. He did not know then, as we learnt years later from anthropological studies, that in rural India nobody eats with members of a caste lower than their own. Eating lines are the rule even between twice-born Hindus, let alone Untouchables like ourselves. Prem Singh, who did not mind eating cakes and sandwiches with me, could not afford to be seen eating at the same table with us in his village. Finding suitable husbands for his sisters would have been jeopardized. Extracting a sizeable dowry for himself might have become difficult. In any event, he would have had to undergo expensive purification rites. The house in which we were entertained was not his family house, but the council's office. Maurice might be a VIP; his coming to the village a great honour for Prem Singh's family, but homes had to be protected against pollution.

Maurice said I should eat the curry, he would eat the chapattis and a gooey rice stew dotted with almonds and grit. The curry was exceedingly spicy. It was so dark with all those people blocking the entrance that I could not tell what I was eating, except it burnt. There was a small bowl with an even spicier curry, so spicy that tears streamed down my face. Remembering that the eyes of His Majesty the King Emperor were on me, I ate stoically. For the sake of the British Raj in India I finished the food, grateful for the penumbra which hid my tears. Prem Singh later said that the smaller bowl contained pickled peppers, and that even the best of Jats would have eaten of it only sparingly.

As soon as we finished eating Prem Singh said it was time to go back. Back in the boot of the car I felt dizzy. My tongue was swollen, I was sweating profusely. All I remember from the return journey is a scorching stomach upset which forced me to get out of the car every so often. By the time we reached the Club I was racked with fever. Maurice had to get a doctor. I was unwell for three days. To make amends Maurice had his files sent to the Club and stayed in bed as my hot-water bottle.

Another occasion when the crushing weight of the Imperial Mantle fell upon the Republican shoulders was less traumatic, if more frightening.

We had been invited to shoot. The men had guns, the women were beating, deployed at intervals to replace dogs. I stood in a recently ploughed field at the edge of a hamlet. The villagers were watching. I had been told to walk straight ahead parallel with a pond, making as much noise as possible. Suddenly, to my horror, a gigantic water-buffalo, steam shooting from its nostrils, charged at me. The earth trembled under its hooves. The grunts were terrifying. I was about to run for dear life when I remembered the watching villagers. A representative of the King Emperor could not be seen panicking. The British Raj was a miraculous mirage, a confidence trick. Only a handful of men ruled India. Noblesse obliged. I walked slowly, looking at the ground not to see the beast, singing, very out of tune, the beginning of the Marseillaise, like a broken record. I was so scared I could not remember what came after 'Allons enfants de la patrie, allons enfants de la patrie, allons enfants . . . ' I could hear my heart pounding . . . that monster was going to gore me. As it turned out, that superhuman effort to preserve appearances saved me. Had I run I would most probably have fallen because of the ridge in the ground. I had, inadvertently, come between the cow and her calf. By the time mother and child were reunited I was no longer in the way. My distaste of water-buffaloes dates back to that morning when I behaved like a pukka memsahib. After 1947 I could be myself. Thank God for the Transfer of Power!

10

Grace, glitter, giggles

Maurice assures me I am a born memsahib. He may be right, but even a born memsahib has to learn. So much of the jargon was, as with boarding-school lingo, esoteric. What made learning particularly difficult was the absence of a book with the meaning of those abbreviations which kept intruding. One could not keep interrupting and later one forgot. Malati had already explained that PWD meant Public Works Department. But what did NWFP, IMS, RSS, AICC, stand for? How was I to guess that NWFP means North West Frontier Province and IMS Indian Medical Service while RSS stands for Rashtrya Sevak Sangh, a militant Hindu Right Wing organisation, and AICC for All India Congress Committee? To make confusion more confusing there were the short ones. UP, CP, IP, IG . . . UP standing for United Provinces, CP for Central Provinces, while IP did not stand for a Province but for Indian Police. Then too, there was Section 144 which everybody but me knew to mean that under that section of the Criminal Procedure Code processions and the assembly of more than four people could be banned. Like Urdu, all this jargon had to be learnt. And learning took time.

My new Urdu teacher was middle-aged and dedicated. A good Muslim, he did not drink or smoke. He chewed betel-nuts and pan instead. His lips and his tongue were the same colour as his greying hair, dyed red to look like the Prophet's.

Fat and tall, he always began the lesson by preparing his provision of pan. The ritual fascinated me. From a small silver box divided into layers and compartments he took out pan leaves, one at a time, smeared each with white lime and a red paste, packed it with betel-nut shavings and small aromatic seeds, always in the same order, then with amazing dexterity, he made small triangular bundles which he pinned down with a clove. He chewed his creations in the same way as Americans chew gum: continuously, only breaking into English when he got so excited that I could not follow.

From him I learnt a fair amount of basic, as distinct from high-flown, Urdu. I remained illiterate because Urdu is like Arabic, Hebrew and shorthand. Many abbreviations, few vowels. One has to know what one is reading to be able to decipher it. I could never master shorthand. Whereas Prem Singh's teaching had been from a primer, Abdul Khader ad-libbed. Once he realized I had a block against the script he gave up writing to concentrate on conversation.

A fanatical Muslim Leader, Abdul Khader was frequently in attendance at Jinnah's residence. He was a typist in the Central Secretariat and when Jinnah was in town, used to volunteer his services in Pakistan's cause. I learnt a great deal about Indian politics from him. He came from Lucknow and was proud of being Muslim.

Maurice had many Muslims amongst his friends and colleagues but they were far too urbane, or reticent, to speak of Hindus the way Adbul Khader and the majority of Jinnah's followers did. What I learnt from him provided me, once I became a journalist, with much background for the way Pakistan looked at India.

According to Abdul Khader it was Sir Sayyid Ahmad Khan who laid the foundation-stone of Pakistan, way back in 1875, when he created the Muslim College, later to become a University, at Aligarh; 'Sir Sayyid was very far sighted. He realised even then that one day your people would leave

India and that they would leave it as a functioning democracy. Democracy, Sir Sayyid kept telling the Muslims, means one man one vote. See what a clever genius he was! And since Hindus are in the majority, Sir Sayyid argued that the Muslims must have a State of their own. Otherwise they would be ruled by Hindus.' Abdul Khader's jet of ochre saliva landed on the gravel in front of our verandah as he exploded: 'We are not idol-worshippers like Hindus! We believe in one God: Allah. We do not drink cow's urine like Hindus! And we pray inside our mosques, not in the streets where they make a lot of noise around idols and disturb people at prayer in mosques. We do not make blood sacrifices and we are Alkitabis, people of the Book. Our religion is very much like yours. We do not have thousands of Gods and we do not worship trees or stones. And because they worship the cow and drink its urine they go amok when we feast on cow-meat to celebrate Id. Before you, the British came, it was we, the Muslims, who ruled India! Only a few years ago, in my father's time, Hindus had to get off the sidewalk to make room for Muslims. The thought that Gandhi, that naked fakir as your great Winston Churchill calls him, will rule us after you go is intolerable! I would rather be dead!' Another copious jet of ochre saliva underscored this assertion before he repeated: 'I would rather be dead than be ruled by urine-drinking idol-worshippers!'

We must have been in Delhi for a couple of months when we were given a married quarter. A most welcome change. Our new home was at the end of a row with, in effect, a private garden facing a spacious verandah which ran the length of a good sized drawing-room and a comfortable bedroom. Like everything else in Maurice's India, the furniture was PWD - solid, pedestrian. Fortunately we had enough pictures to decorate the walls and I managed to enliven both rooms at practically no cost. For lamp-shades I used sieves made of bamboo and rice-straw. They only cost 4 annas each - fourpence of those days - and their webbing cast pleasing shadows. Moghul prints on cheap cotton sacking made colourful cushion covers and curtains.

For a bedspread I found in Old Delhi's Thieves' Market a beautifully embroidered wedding curtain from Sind. Indian antiques were not in demand in those days. Few Europeans appreciated them and most fashion-minded Indians looked to the West for inspiration.

There were exceptions like my friend Leela Row, the wife of Harish Dayal, an ICS colleague of Maurice's. Leela Row, she insisted on keeping her maiden name, had been a tennis champion; she even played at Wimbledon, I believe. Educated in Paris she had given demonstrations of Indian dancing at the Musée Guimet. Eccentric, extrovert, she had written a small manual to explain the meaning of the various ornaments, poses and gestures of Bharatanatyam - the dancing style which, like so much of Indian art, is dedicated to worship. I found her little book, graphically illustrated, a most useful introduction. It was not just because of her French background that Leela was so different from most Indian ICS wives of her generation. Like me, she loved Indian textiles, and wore ancient saris and jewels which had belonged to dancing girls.

Her rooms were typically Indian, scantily furnished with low chairs and sofas. A magnificent swinging platform hung from the ceiling of her drawing-room by four bronze chains, lavishly decorated with mythological beasts.

In one corner, hidden under a pile of cushions, there was a large teak chest in which she kept her saris - hundreds of them. Sometimes she opened that chest and showed me her treasures, neatly folded. From her I learnt to tell Murshidabad silk, Benares brocade, Patoli weaves, Chanderi cottons, Dacca muslins, Tanjore taffetas, Mysore shot-silks . . . Fluent in Sanskrit, French, Marathi and English, Leela was vegetating in Delhi. No longer a tennis champion, she had given up dancing, brooded over the past and missed her mother who lived in Bombay. The only child of a well-known doctor married to a Sanskrit scholar-blue-stocking, Leela had come back to India before the war. Independent minded, a rabid feminist, like her mother, she would only marry for love.

'What a beauty!' I exclaimed, catching a glimpse of a deep red silk and gold brocade sari at the bottom of the chest. 'Do show it to me, please'.

She had already slammed the lid shut saying with sudden violence: 'I *hate* red!' Yet she opened the chest, slowly, if reluctantly, and took out the sari. It was a temple sari from South India, the kind used for Brahmin weddings. After putting it back and closing the chest she exploded; 'I hate that sari. I feel like burning it every time I see it. You know, Taya, one does burn saris to recover the gold, and there is a lot of gold in that horrid sari.' Noticing the expression on my face she added: 'It is my tunique de Nessus, ma chère, my first wedding sari. The sari I wore to marry Khania, the man I loved.'

Shortly after her return to Bombay Leela had met the young Indian Civil Servant and fallen in love. On her wedding day, after all the preliminaries had been completed, as the guests who had assembled in Dr Row's garden were waiting for the betrothed couple to step out so that the priest could perform the sacred rites over the ritual fire, Leela's fiancé went stark raving mad and tried to rape her. There was a struggle. Servants held the young man while Dr Row injected a sedative. The sedative was well-known and reputed harmless. Leela's fiancé dropped dead. Laughing bitterly she said: 'You see, Taya, I had become that thing which amuses foreigners in the matrimonial columns of our newspapers: "a virgin widow." There was a big scandal. Poor Father.'

When I told Maurice about Khania's dramatic death he burst out. 'How absolutely dreadful! Poor Leela. I knew Khania. We were together in Sholapur. He was such a nice fellow - so gentle. I knew he was dead but I did not know why.'

Soon after Leela married Harish. 'A good man, also ICS. From a good family with another brother, Rajeshwar, in the ICS. What more could I ask for? A woman cannot remain single in India. Do you know, sometimes I ask myself whether I do not have the evil eye. We have already been married for a long time and have no children. Mind you, I am not sorry, I don't particularly care for children. I am an intellectual like Mother; Mother is a Pandita, an Honoured Sanskrit Scholar. Yes, I am an intellectual like Mother, and a sportswoman, not at all the maternal type. What I mind about is my Art, my sports and my Sanskrit. But poor Harish would love children. Am I cursed with barrenness or is it he?'

Leela had no luck. A keen mountaineer, like her mother, when Harish became India's Ambassador to Nepal, Leela decided to beat the altitude record for husband and wife. No mountaineer and too busy to start from base camp, Harish joined her by helicopter. After a day's climb he began to cough. Their guide sent for help. Harish died of pulmonary oedema. For three days Leela stayed alone on a narrow ledge. Alone in a tent with her husband's corpse. The last time I saw her she was writing epic poems and traditional plays in Sanskrit.

My first Indian friend was soon followed by a second. Like Leela's, Zeenat's was an arranged marriage. Like Leela's, Zeenat's husband was in the ICS, but my two friends, though equally wilful, were as different as the Equator is from the Poles. Leela, a non-conformist Hindu, was attracted to Buddhism. Zeenat was a selectively practising Muslim. Leela was older than her husband. Zeenat's husband was nearly old enough to be her father. Leela, for an Indian of those days had married old. Zeenat married at seventeen. Leela's education had been unusually broad, extensive and unconventional. Zeenat had tumbled from purdah and a convent into the matrimonial bed. Leela's turned out to be an arranged marriage, Zeenat's a love match.

'I have invited Azim to come to tea with his new bride. I am very fond of him. His father, a Muslim landowner from the South, had a Scottish wife, that's probably why Azim waited such a long time to get married. His wife is a Pathan, the daughter of an important politician who keeps his daughters and his first wife in purdah.'

'Why his first wife? Has he got many?'

'Only two. He recently married again, a young lady doctor from a wealthy landowning family from Sind. It made quite a ripple. We expect poligamy only from Princes.'

'Will she speak English?' I was acutely aware of the limitations of my Urdu. Maurice laughed.

'Of course she'll speak English. I bet you that in her convent English was the medium of instruction, and she was probably a boarder. I wouldn't at all be suprised if she spoke English better than Pushtu or Urdu. In any case she has to speak English with Azim. His Urdu is not very fluent and it often happens when people from different parts of India get married that they have only English in common. That is one reason why English education is at such a high premium and why it will continue to be one of India's main languages long after we are gone. You must have noticed how many Indians speak good English even if, like Prem Singh and Abdul Khander, they have never set foot outside India. It all goes back to Macauley.' Maurice was trying to convince me that the British had done as good a linguistic job in India as the French in their colonies.

'Maybe there are lots of Indians who speak good English, but they are the elite. English has not percolated down at all; not even to the artisan class. I had to talk Hindustani or Urdu to the electrician who came to fix the plug; the gardener does not understand English . . . We did a much better

Zeenat and Azim are not their real names.

The author at work. Unless there is a mess on my table I cannot concentrate. *(Photo: Derek Bayes)*

My brother a *Life Magazine* photographer made me look my best when Maurice asked for my photo. I married him after nine years' correspondence having met him once.

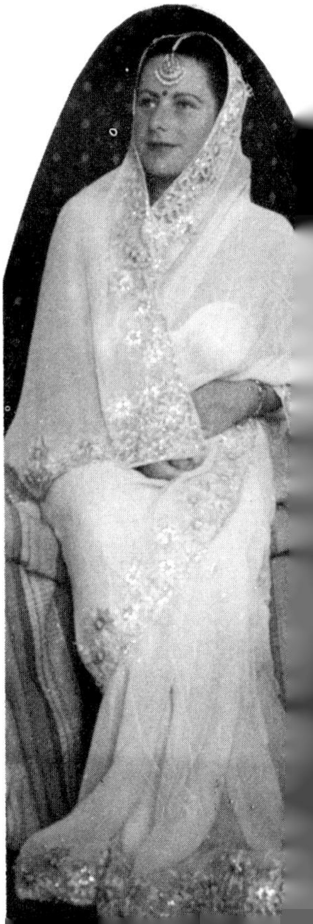

One of my beautiful Indian friends lent me glamorous saris. I wore one at the last Viceregal Reception, even though I had forty new evening gowns in my trousseau.

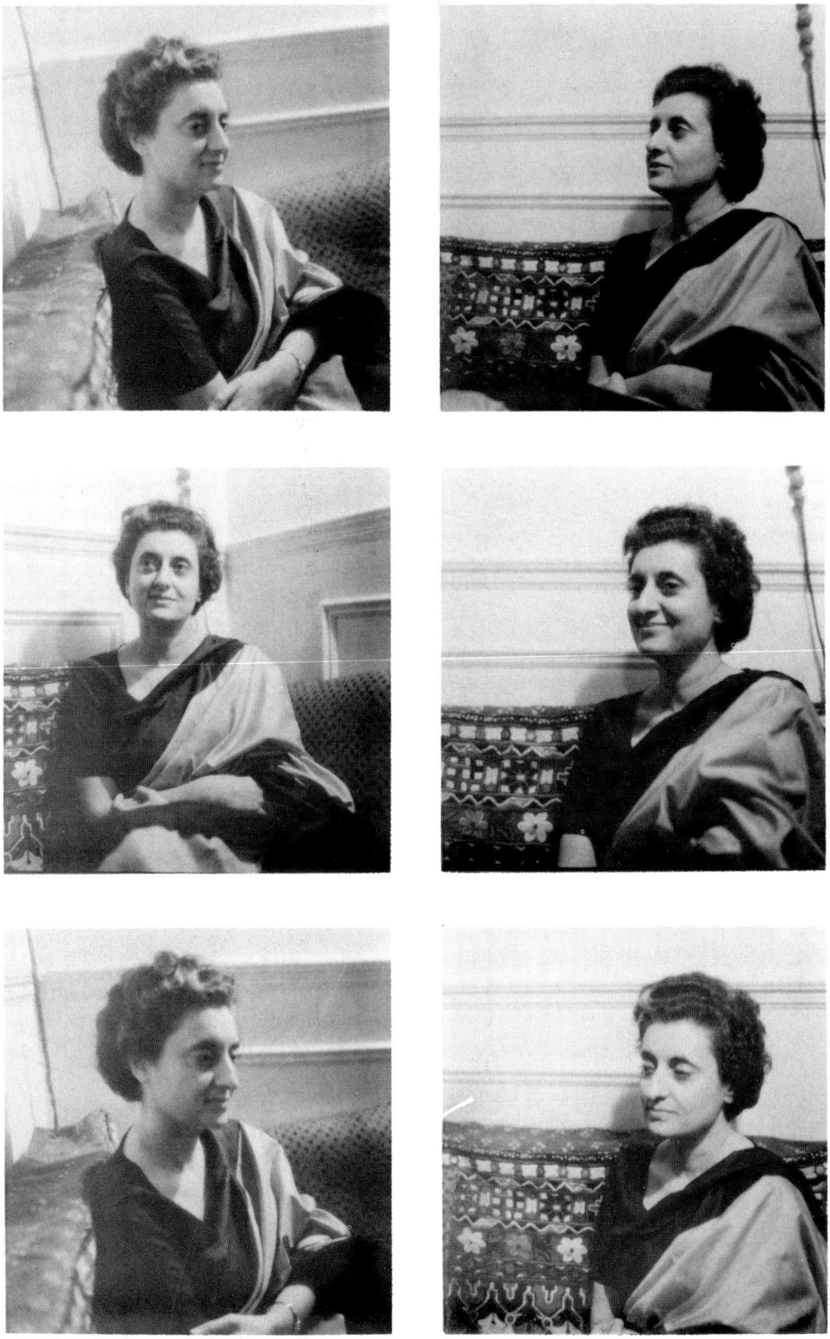

Snaps I took of my friend Indira Gandhi, still shy and diffident in those days, and before she became Prime Minister.

Peasants from Rajasthan. I fell in love with those flared skirts - 28 yards at the hem - and had one made during my first trip there. *(Photo: Press Information Bureau, Government of India)*

The Maharajah of Jaipur. Ayesha, his number three beautiful wife, was a great friend of Premy, our son's godmother. *(Photo: Press Information Bureau, Government of India)*

A splendid character from Rajasthan.
(Photo: Press Information Bureau, Government of India)

For Nehru and Mountbatten it had been love at first sight, a love which included Lady Mountbatten. *(Photo: Press Information Bureau, Government of India)*

Bharat Natyam dancer, not unlike the girl who kept us enthralled for a whole night in the Maharajah of Jaipur's guest house. *(Photo: Press Information Bureau, Government of India)*

Tribal dancers from Orissa. Nehru never missed an opportunity to stress India's diversity. His cultural programmes went on for hours. I once had to wake up Mountbatten by tripping over his leg.

Hyderabadi tribal dancers. *(Photo: Press Information Bureau, Government of India)*

Sadar Patel, Deputy Prime Minister of India, a great patriot whose pique at a paper on the viability of Pakistan cost my husband a whole year's compensation for loss of career.

Mahatma Gandhi during one of his fasts. Meticulously punctual, Gandhi took infinite pains to put his visitors at ease.

Patel and Nehru. The two men did not get on. A couple of years later I accompanied Nehru to Patel's cremation. 'Tell Nehru not to cry,' our five-year old son told me. At this India's Prime Minister burst out laughing.

Mahomed Ali Jinnah, the Father of Pakistan. He disowned his only child because she did not marry a Muslim; yet he himself was an agnostic, had married a Parsee, did not know Arabic and was totally Western. *(Photo: Press Information Bureau, Government of India)*

Muslim refugees waiting to be evacuated to Pakistan during the riots of Partition.

My son and I three months after our miraculous recovery.

Mahatma Gandhi talking to villagers. Churchill once called him a 'naked Fakir'.

Mahatma Gandhi in conference with Pandit Nehru *(Photo: Press Information Bureau, Government of India)*

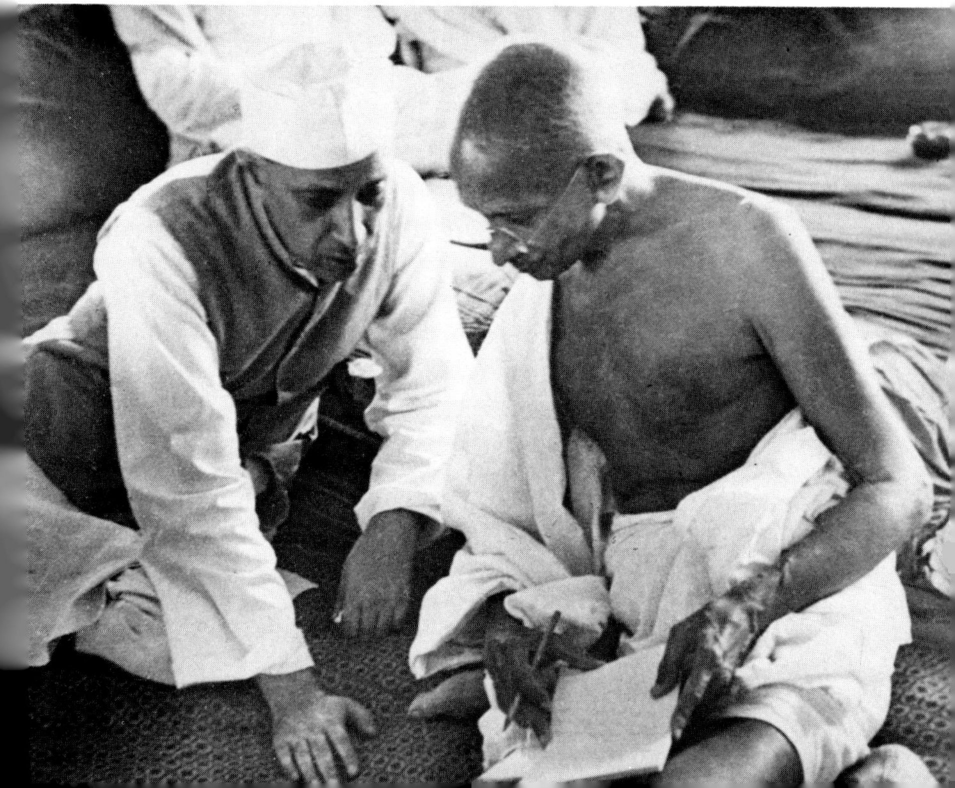

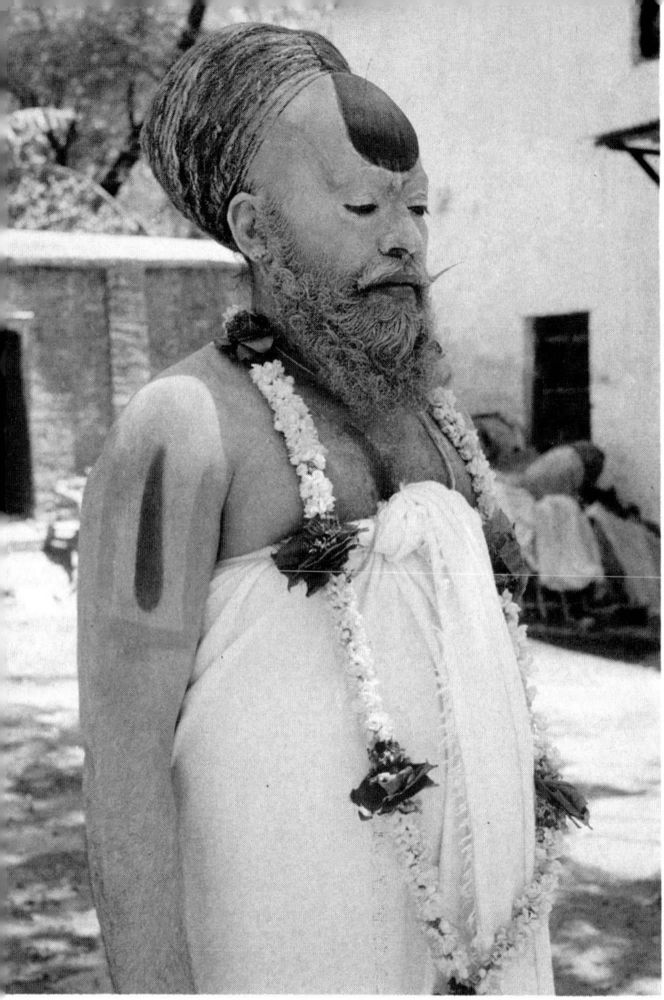

A Fakir - An ash and paint-smeared Hindu religious mendicant. *(Photo: Press Information Bureau, Government of India.)*

My first journalistic effort. Watching Muslim women going to vote during the Referendum in Peshawar for the correspondent of the BBC who paid me twenty rupees (£1.50).

Muslim woman refugee in burkha with her child on her lap. Like millions of others she was waiting to be evacuated to Pakistan, in her case by rail.

Nehru who was not a good father. However he was a doting grand-father and took a great deal of interest in schemes for children.*(Photo: Press Information Bureau, Government of India)*

job in Morocco, Senegal, even in Haiti . . . ' This was a sore point on which we would never agree.

Zeenat's entrance - there is no other word for it - was unforgettable.

Carried on the billows of a magnificent skirt with kilometres of flimsy red and gold silk, layered, gathered, adorned, overlaid with gold sequins, she was lavishly bedecked with glittering jewelry. A red and gold Christmas tree. The sumptuous extravagance of her attire outshining her beauty. Very tall, slim, curvaceous. Huge green eyes, almond shaped, with long black lashes. Cascades of silky red-black hair set off an extraordinarily dusty-pink complexion. Her hands, admirably shaped, with long tapering fingers and elegant nails still bore the auspicious bridal patterns dyed with henna-paste, and her slender wrists, generously laden with bangles, chimed every time she moved her expressive hands. Three-tiered bell-shaped bejewelled earrings dangled halfway to her shoulders, matching an elaborate display on her neck and chest and a large pendant which covered half her high forehead, hanging between perfectly arched eyebrows. A shimmering ball of fire, Zeenat shot rays from those enormous eyes - an oriental Hedy Lamarr, bursting with temperament.

What a pity, I thought, she is overdressed, overdecorated. And red so unbecoming. This wonderful complexion calls for blacks, whites, muted pastels, even peacock blue. Red, never.

While Azim and Maurice talked shop, Zeenat confided she had, against Azim's advice, put on her wedding outfit.

'When Azim said you were French, I decided I must look my very best, especially since it is the first time I am going on a visit now that I am out of purdah. And what, I said to Azim, do men know about clothes? I hope, Mrs Zinkin, you like my gharara. Our women wear pyjamas, kamises and dupatas - shoulder scarves - but for marriage we wear a gharara instead of pyjamas. Don't you think it's beautiful?'

To show off the fantastic width of her ankle-length skirt, she twirled, fanning out, inverted flower.

Before taking leave Azim, who had been watching us, asked if I could lend some good books to his wife. Delighted by Zeenat's lack of inhibition I said I would. She already had confessed, between cucumber sandwiches and fruit cake, that while at boarding school she had felt the *call.*

'I had a real vocation and wanted to become a nun. The only reason I did not pursue my vocation was that it would have broken Mummy's heart, especially with daddy marrying again. Perhaps it is my fate not to be a nun. Inch Allah!' The incongruity of that wild beauty shaving her hair struck me so forcibly that I burst out laughing. Inch Allah indeed.

For a short while I took Zeenat in hand. Years later, whenever we met in the world's capitals, we never failed to rake up Dostoyevsky from my reading list, a list the nuns would not have approved. Extremely intelligent, though undisciplined, an amazing memory, tremendous charm and a kittenish lack of sophistication compensated by himalayan self-assurance, Zeenat was a joy to be with. She never stayed still, always looking for fun. She was always remarkably fair-minded, a virtue which became exceedingly rare as Hindu-Muslim tension increased. Zeenat's fair-mindedness was not confined to religion or politics. She alone in her family had befriended her 'stepmother' as she called her father's second wife.

'Do you know, Taya, the other day I rang up my stepmother and invited her to lunch. It is not her fault if she fell in love with Daddy. Put yourself in her place. I would *hate* to be a second wife! I would insist on divorce first. But she understands how Mummy would feel at being divorced. True, Daddy lives with my step and has pensioned Mummy off in Lahore. But still, everybody knows that she is a second wife. And she is very educated, a practising doctor. I like her a lot and I am damned if I am going to boycott her. After all she makes Daddy happy. Mummy is old-fashioned and retiring, she actually *likes* being in purdah! I suppose Daddy needed more stimulating company. You know, Mummy is beautiful, even now that she is quite old, I think she is over forty, and my step is not at all beautiful, but she is full of beans and very nice. We are becoming friends.'

All my memories of Zeenat are bigger than life. It was she, years later in London, who taught our son to dance the Twist and beat us at scrabble, scoring 145 points in one go. Once, when I was staying with her in Karachi, she took me to an official dance and I amused myself counting the number of Ambassadors - Karachi was then the capital - who were at her feet. It was during that visit that she told me she would learn to play bridge because she was afraid of a 'middle-aged, plump, quiet, European mouse' with whom Azim played regularly at the Club. Muslim women, she declared, were at their husbands' mercy. Suppose Azim were to follow her father's example and marry that mouse, where would she be? It did not take Zeenat long to become one of the Club's best players. Instead of spending evenings on the dance floor she beat her husband at cards and frightened the mouse away. Her fears were imaginary. Azim is not that sort of man.

In those early days when I lent her books and she lent me saris, I often cycled to the little hotel at the back of Connaught Circus which was her home. Zeenat preferred a hotel in the centre of town to the Gymkhana Club's quiet residential area.

'If you come before lunch, you will have to go to the dining-room without me. It is Ramadan; I am fasting. We have to fast a whole month from sunrise to sunset.' I arrived after lunch to find my friend nibbling a box of chocolates. 'I was hungry. So long as I preserve appearances it is OK. All that stuff is bigotry, hypocrisy. Good Muslims don't drink or smoke - in theory that is. In practice a lot of them smoke and even more drink. A good Muslim must treat all his wives exactly the same. That is what is written in the Koran.

But how can they? Mummy is in purdah in Lahore. Purdah of her own choice, but purdah just the same. Daddy does not visit her. My step goes with him everywhere. So much for rules.' Squatting on her bed under the ceiling-fan, legs crossed, her hair afloat in the wind, she went on regaling herself. 'Have a chocolate.' The box was almost empty. 'Have some pistachios, I love them.' With the claws of her long nails lacquered dark red she pranged the nuts open. 'Revlon,' she smiled as I watched her hands. 'My step brought it back, with matching lipstick, from London. Nice, don't you think. As a matter of fact I would see her much more often if I was not afraid this would hurt Mummy. In India one can never keep secrets, walls and servants have ears, and ears have tongues and tongues have imagination.' In order that I could better admire her nail varnish she stuck her hand in front of my eyes. It was then that I noticed the scars on her wrist.

'What have you been doing?' There were many scars, some faded, some recent, one still red. Zeenat tossed back her head and laughed.

'I have a fiery temper, like Daddy. But I have hit, by accident, on an infallible trick to control myself. I always wear at least a couple of glass bangles. When I feel that I am going to explode with rage I break a bangle and slash my skin. Glass bangles are very cheap. I have hundreds. The pain, above all the need to stop the blood making a mess, takes my anger away. I have been doing this for years. See my other wrist.' It had more scars.

'Isn't it too drastic?'

'Not really. Better hurt oneself than throw something and perhaps kill somebody. I am a Pathan. Pathans can be ferocious. Besides one never really hurts oneself badly. But let me show you my collection of bangles. I have a little woman from Rajasthan who comes once a month with a whole lot more.' Inside a small leather suitcase, neatly arranged by colour, there were hundreds of glass bangles, threaded in rows, upon velvet covered poles, as slender as Zeenat's wrists.

'How do you get them on? They are so much smaller than your hands and glass, especially when it is so thin, is very brittle?'

'It's very simple. Ever since I can remember as a child, I have had bangles. Of course not glass. To thread bangles you have to fold your hand so that the knuckles of the little finger and the thumb meet. It's a matter of practice. Mummy says you can always tell a woman of breeding by her bangles.' Zeenat was undoubtedly a woman of breeding.

'That's nothing. You should see my eldest sister - the beautiful one. Her bangles are much smaller than mine.' She showed me a photograph of her sister. 'She is the beauty of the family. Her eyes are grey and much bigger than mine, her nose is small, straight and she has teeth like pearls.' Zeenat's aristocratic nose was fairly prominent and divided her face into slightly unequal parts. Her teeth needed straightening. Yet she was by far the fairer of the two. I had heard so much about her sister's beauty that I was thoroughly disappointed when I did meet her. Perfectly cut features. Admirable teeth. A very light skin. A face so devoid of expression that it faded into lifeless insignificance. A perfect statue.

With Zeenat it was not just the looks but the babble, the inner fire, which made her irresistible. When the American Government invited a group of administrators from newly independent countries to visit the United States for a study tour, Azim took Zeenat with him. He was not alone in bringing his wife. But he alone was repeatedly faced by the most embarrassing situations. After the group's visit to General Motors, its President insisted on presenting Zeenat with the latest model, a large black limousine, the first car I saw with electrically operated windows. Zeenat returned from America with a refrigerator, which due to the difference of voltage, created problems, as did an impressive hi-fi cabinet and an air-conditioner, to mention only bulkier tokens of male admiration. Wherever the State Department sent them, she was showered with gifts.

She was such fun to be with that I missed her greatly when Azim sent her back to Lahore to be with her mother for the birth of their child, as was the custom.

'You wait and see. I won't be long. As soon as the midwife and the doctor say it is safe to travel. I love Mummy but I don't want to be away from Azim for long. I love Delhi and I hate purdah.' Unfortunately, time dragged on and there was no sign of labour. To beat the clock she skipped a rope, without success. Fed up she decided to act.

'You will never guess what I did.' She was glowing with satisfaction at being back. 'I put on my wedding gharara, remember the red and gold outfit, and all the wedding jewelry and I made up, as loudly as a dancing girl. I am so tall that in my gharara I did not show. I sneaked out of the house and went to the Mall, walking slowly, smiling at strangers. A lot of GIs are stationed in Lahore. A young one, nice looking, stopped his jeep and we had a little chat. He offered to take me for a ride. "Let's go far away to the hills" I said and kept egging him on. "Faster, go faster, I simply adore speed". You see, Taya, the road to the hills is full of pot holes. We were shaken like dice. It got so bad one could not talk for fear of biting one's tongue. We must have gone quite a way when labour started. I told him to drive back to Lahore and take me to the hospital. He thought I was joking . . . we just made it. Our son was born in the jeep inside the hospital compound. I had to have stitches, he was born so fast.' Before I could express shocked disapproval Zeenat added with blatant innocence that it was all my fault for lending her Anna Karenina and Madame Bovary; 'it put ideas in my head. By the way, Taya, do you think that GI will pick women up again?'

Motherhood did not alter Zeenat's looks or affect her life style. She had brought back from Lahore a slave to act as nursemaid.

'Ayesha was born in Mummy's house, the daughter of a slave. Mummy brought her up and trained her. She can do everything: cook, embroider, wash, iron, sew, massage, make designs with henna paste. She is like a younger sister to me, absolutely devoted. We don't pay her, but she does not need money - she gets everything from us and knows that we will look after her always. In due course Mummy, or I, will find her a husband and give her a trousseau.'

With the baby and Ayesha, Zeenat's life in the hotel was crowded but there was such a housing shortage they did not move.

Maurice had been offered a temporary house. When he took me to see it I flatly refused to move in. Two small communicating rooms, a small bathroom with a thunder-box, one cold-water tap above a hole in the ground, a tiny kitchen with a kerosene stove, no fans, no electricity. Petromaxes for lighting and one narrow verandah in the front, facing no man's land on the outskirts of New Delhi. I was pregnant.

Such a house was out of the question.

'But, Darling, if I refuse, I lose my turn on the waiting list for the C-class house to which we are entitled. I must accept.'

'And I absolutely refused to move in. The floor is made of beaten earth, the roof of corrugated sheeting. Prefabs may be fine in London but here, with the climate and no electricity, no fans, no WC and far from everything. Out of the question.'

It was then that I had a brainwave.

'Didn't you say the other day that Akhil something, that fellow who shares your office, keeps complaining because his wife hates living in a hotel. Perhaps he could take that house in your name?'

Thus began my friendship with Akhil. There were fourteen of them living in our 'house'. Akhil had been married to the heiress of a minor Bengali princely family. Used at home to having twenty-eight ayahs to look after her small person, she had brought many servants with her.

'How can fourteen people fit into two small rooms and a small verandah?'

Akhil explained they had no furniture, only bedding rolls and two string cots which stood against the wall during the day. The baby slept in a hammock suspended in mid-air. Junior to Maurice, Akhil belonged to the Audit and Accounts Service, an All India Service which ranked second after the the ICS.

11

Somerset Maugham tout pur

Life in Delhi was official. Hierarchical. Stuffy. Snobbish. Before the war thirty-nine administrators above the rank of Assistant Secretary manned the Government of India. By 1945 their number had multiplied. To meet the demands of the War Effort the Central Government had drawn upon the Provinces, the armed Forces and on business. Dilution had petrified hierarchy.

Thanks to the Warrant of Precedence India's hierarchy was as complicated as it was crystal clear. The Warrant of Precedence, that voluminous document rating official jobs in order of importance, laid down, with Mosaic rigour, who came ahead of whom. A Member of the Viceroy's Council ranked number nine, a Major General number twenty-nine, a Collector number forty-three, and so on. At official functions, especially at meals, people were seated strictly in accordance with their rating in the Warrant of Precedence. Wives in particular kept a hawk's eye on seating lest somebody less important than themselves, or their husbands, was placed nearer the hosts. The job being rated, who filled it did not matter. The Collector could be British, Indian or Anglo-Indian, a member of the ICS or someone promoted from the Provincial Service; all that mattered, for his place at the table, was his being a Collector.

The ICS enjoyed a subtly built-in advantage. ICS posts ranked ahead of equivalent posts in other All India Services.

Promotion was faster in the ICS. In any given job members of the ICS were younger, and many of the top administrative posts were reserved for them. Maurice, as a Deputy Secretary to the Government of India, ranked thirty-one between a Brigadier and a Major General.

Problems only arose with non-officials. Where to sit a businessman? Usually at the bottom of the table. Businessmen, 'boxwallahs' as they were called, were not quite U. In Bombay, or Calcutta, if he was the head of a major firm, he might, unofficially, fare a little better.

But the Warrant of Precedence was not everything. There was snobbery as well. The rich young man in a British cavalry regiment might be sought after even if he was boneheaded. The Anglo-Indian Collector might have nasty remarks made behind his back. I was often told that some of Maurice's Indian colleagues under-paid and beat their servants and lived on rice and curry. Snobbery got steadily worse as one went down the social scale. British Managers of one of the British banks could not, as Maurice had already explained, marry before thirty and if his superiors thought the bride unsuitable - say Anglo-Indian - they would sack him on the spot. Tea-plantation bosses some times behaved like bankers.

The ICS, by contrast, married whom they liked and the Service saw to it that wives were accepted be they Anglo-Indian, domiciled Europeans, or daughters of Police Sergeants. Such a wife might be gossiped about behind her back, but to be fully accepted all she had to do was to have personality, like Marie Longford, née Thompson.

The Thompsons from Kanpur were 'domiciled Europeans', who, though of European stock, had made India their home. Some domiciled families, like Bihar indigo planters, were rich and important but most were descended from police sergeants, NCOs or the drivers of mail trains. The Thompsons were successful. The boy became an industrialist. Two of the girls married into the ICS, the third - a raving beauty - married for the third time, none other than the Duke of Sutherland. I never saw the Duchess whose pictures used to enliven the glossies but I saw a good deal of her sister Marie, especially after our son was born.

Like Molly Tymms, Marie was a natural. No chips on her bony shoulders, no snobbishness, no pretence. Take-me-as-you-find-me Marie was middle-aged, thin as a stick, invariably dressed in home-made things run up by a verandah tailor devoid of talent or inspiration. Her skirts, too tight, too short, exposed knobbly knees. Usually in slippers, she wore shoes only when 'going out'. A compulsive knitter and smoker - two fingers dyed nicotine mahogany, she was warm, hospitable, matter-of-fact and home loving. Her horizon began - and ended - with Jack, her very fat, very able, hard working and hard-drinking husband. His being a Joint Secretary shielded Marie from darting tongues, not that she needed shielding. Marie was quite capable of holding her own. It has been my privilege to witness altercations between that small twig of a woman and servants three times her size. She could outswear the best of them. Her fluency in the vernacular was reminiscent of Kim's hill Ranee whom she resembled from her faith, often justified, in the curative value of herbal decoctions, to the constant use of a voice raspish from excessive smoking. To be with Marie was like inhaling a whiff of fresh air. So much of Delhi's officialdom was soaked in stuffiness.

Not everyone had Marie's strength of character. If they did not have it they were in for trouble, like Loulou who still lies on my conscience, nearly half a century after our fateful meeting.

We had gone to Ziarat, forty-two miles above Quetta, a hill-station perched between eight and nine thousand feet on the way to the Afghan border. Robin, who had shared a flat with Maurice in Bombay, was Deputy Commissioner Upper Sind Frontier. He suggested we spend our summer holiday together. The prospectus he sent us describing the beauties of Baluchistan's Upper Ranges was in flagrant breach of any Trade Descriptions Act. Ziarat is barren, just the odd thorn tree - fodder for camels and donkeys - and juniper bushes. No level ground. 'Tourists', those whose summer residence Ziarat was not, had to stay in clusters of circular huts built on different levels, called roundavels, after South African huts.

Robin met us in Quetta. We travelled with our staff and all the required paraphernalia in a small bus. The road, a disused railway embankment, climbed through arid stony deserts. By the time we reached our destination I was ready for bed. Our roundavel consisted of two bedrooms, one dining-room and a little terrace of levelled ground. Each room stood by itself, one had to walk from one to the other. Abdul was making our bed while Robin's bearer and the driver were unloading the bus, which had to return to Quetta by nightfall, when Marjorie Fell burst upon us, in hot pursuit at the end of the lead of her three dogs.

Marjorie's husband, Douglas, belonged to the Bombay Cadre of the ICS like Maurice and Robin. But unlike them he had gone into the Political Department and was in charge of the Baluch States - now in Pakistan. Marjorie who had known Maurice from his district days was 'dying' to meet his wife, especially because 'You are French, isn't that right?' Robin's bearer conjured drinks while we sat on the little terrace watching the setting sun paint a desolate landscape purple and violet.

'Wait, soon it will turn green and then turquoise and later a luminous topaz,' said Marjorie, sweeping the sky with her hand and, by the way of apology, added 'I paint' before turning to the subject uppermost on her mind. 'I am *so* glad you *are* French! You see, Taya, for a long time we have been having doubts about Loulou. She claims to be French but we all think that she must be Anglo-Indian. The way she keeps throwing French words. And she's always talking about Paris and the Riviera. But she doesn't get letters from France and I'm dashed if I can work out *when* she was in Paris. I can't wait till you meet her'. Loulou was the wife of Douglas's boss. They had three children and were due to come up for the summer.

Inviting us to tea for Sunday, Marjorie left in a clutter of dogs. Robin, obviously amused by her curiosity, said he suspected Marjorie had her knife out for Loulou because her own step-father took pride in being Anglo-Indian.

Next morning we had the visit of Peggy Alington, Ziarat's senior memsahib. Prim, proper, efficient, Peggy had come to invite us to dinner.

'Formal, of course. I shall send one of the servants with a petromax to lead the way. Bring your torches as well. I can lend you some. The path is stony, it gets very dark when the moon is new. And it is so easy to twist an ankle.' With a glance at my distended shape - I was pregnant and huge - she added. 'Don't wear high heels, I would hate for anything to go wrong, we only have a makeshift dispensary up here.' I reassured her, despite appearances, I was only six months gone. 'Colonel Ledgard will be relieved. He caught a glimpse of you as you arrived. A very fine man, the Colonel, and such a good doctor. He is coming to dinner.'

The trek to the Alington bungalow was arduous. Like the half dozen houses built for those who recessed in Ziarat, it stood on a little plateau, some five hundred feet above the tourist roundavels. I found the climb so tiring that I had to stop every couple of minutes to catch my breath and half way up Maurice and Robin had to push me in turn. On reaching the Alington residence - a palace compared to our roundavel - I had to sit outside for a while, I was panting so much.

Dinner was in style. Candlelight. Silver. Lace table-cloth. Starched servants. A crown of chops and caramel custard swathed in spun sugar.

'In Ziarat one has the choice between fat-tailed Dumba sheep and chicken. Beef has to come up specially from Quetta, and fish

- if it arrives - from Karachi. Ice packs seldom last the journey. We have to bury ice - there is no electricity.

Colonel Ledgard, tall, slim, periwinkle-blue eyes, made an excellent impression.

'When my husband arrives, next week, we'll have a feast, said Peggy. 'I have laid on an ice convoy for fish and beef; he's bringing Loulou and her children. Speaking of Loulou, I saw Marjorie walking her dogs this morning, she's quite excited, can hardly wait for you to meet Loulou. I must say I too am curious. That constant use of French words *is* tiresome. There's something odd, perhaps I should say bogus, about her French, especially since you can never pin her down.'

'What do you mean?'

'Well, Taya, for example, she once said she misses walking on the Promenade des Anglais, especially when it is swept by spray from the sea.'

'But that hardly ever happens.'

'That's just it. She immediately changed the subject when I asked if she had lived in Nice the whole year round. I'm afraid I don't really remember concrete examples. But you will see for yourself.'

I felt sorry for Loulou and told Maurice I would say she was French even if she was not. People had been going on about her Frenchness at the swimming pool and at Marjorie's tea party.

'Certainly back her up. But she has probably been asking for it. She need not pretend, if that's what she is doing. With her husband's position she's above all that pettifogging. There will always be gossip in a small station; if it's not one thing, it's another. I am so glad you are having the chance of seeing what district life is like. Except of course that in the District there wouldn't be that many people to talk to - a dozen perhaps, and all working together so that there would be more shop than gossip. But here, with people from all over and with different interests one doesn't get much chance to talk shop - and that leaves gossip. You heard yesterday Robin telling Ledgard how, at the end of the Jacobabad Horse Show, Tony Acton who had fallen in love with the Governor's daughter, lay across the drive to stop them driving off. I think Tony must have been drunk.* Shop and gossip is what fills District leisure, when it is not sports or games.'

Alington arrived with Loulou, her family and the beef. The fish perished en route. The roast beef (and Yorkshire pudding) a treat Ledgard and the Fells had been looking forward to, was leathery. The rest of the meal was fully up to Peggy's impeccable standards. There were just the eight of us, Loulou had not been asked. She was too busy settling in with the children and recovering from the emotions of the journey.

'I must absolutely get something done about that old railway track which we use for a road', said Alington, 'I will put the PWD on to it. We nearly had an accident. A front door swung open and Loulou's youngest fell out. She was darned lucky: she rolled off the embankment and got away with minor scratches and a few bruises. She might have been killed. Loulou, of course, was hysterical. You know how emotional she can be. Latin blood and all that.'

As we left, Marjorie made me promise to call on Loulou the following afternoon. I wanted to wait for an invitation but Marjorie was like a dog with a bone, she would not let go. I kept my promise.

Maurice who had borrowed an ancient and bulky copy of the *Sind Gazetteer*, refused to accompany me, on the pretext he had to finish it. Robin wanted to stay with Samuel Butler, his favourite author. 'The Way of All Flesh' held greater attractions than a ladies' tea. So I went alone.

Without anybody to push me I found the climb exhausting.

*Forty years later. I asked Tony and the Governor's daughter about this. Both denied it absolutely.

The thin mountain air, the heat of the afternoon, my swollen body, were turning what I had decided would be an errand of mercy into a calvary. I had found a way of defusing the situation and was rehearsing mentally how I would indicate to Loulou that I would back her up.

I was so short of breath that I could hear my heart thumping in my head. By the side of the bungalow, in the shade of a tree, they were sitting: Marjorie, Peggy, with children playing at their feet. Standing by a trestle table, a handsome woman with a rich head of jet black hair was sorting apricots. Marjorie, who had obviously been on the look out, rushed towards me, announcing at the top of her voice:

'There she is! Loulou, meet Taya, she too is French.' Apricots dropped from Loulou's hands, rolled on the trestle table and fell to the ground. She said in a toneless voice:

'I am Italian, not French.'

Her husband divorced her a few months later.

ICS solidarity would have protected her had she admitted being Anglo-Indian from the start.

12

Glamour, glory, guts

But for the wife of the self-appointed riding instructor, some aspects of Indian life would have remained closed to me. Phipps used to boast of his wife's knowledge even more than of his horsemanship.

'Just wait till Christmas, when you will meet Stella. She is coming to spend a week in Delhi!' Like a child with an Advent Calendar, he kept counting the days. 'She arrives tomorrow! I know she will be exhausted. Such a long journey, so much soot on the Toofan Mail! But the day after, I know that she will love to meet you. Come to tea. I'll leave the office early.'

Phipps had spoken of his professorial wife with such veneration that I did not know what to expect. I was taken aback.

Petite, extremely soignée, in a dress of timelessly tight simplicity redeemed by the eccentric gorgeousness of its shimmering textile, Professor Stella Kramrisch had enormous luminous dark eyes. She must have been stunning during her youth from which she retained the grace typical of ballet dancers. Her English was accented with Germanicisms. She made it abundantly clear that she did not enjoy my coming to tea and expected me to leave as soon as I had swallowed the cucumber sandwiches and the biscuits provided by the Club. Phipps did most of the talking.

'Taya has interesting things, she must show you her Russian paintings, her ikon, her Picasso and her Toulouse-Lautrec.'

'Etchings,' I hurriedly corrected. There was no stopping Phipps. 'And there is that antique Chantilly mantilla. You will simply love it. It is stunning over a black dress. It is a present from someone whose ancestor received it from Marie-Antoinette.' This was greeted with a flicker of interest.

Tea over, Pofessor Kramrisch got up:

'All right. Show me now.' Phipps stayed behind to work. 'Government business cannot wait, you know.' Professor Kramrisch walked briskly, spoke sparingly. She viewed my treasures like a valuer. 'That is good, that's rubbish. Interesting.' She did not sit down. 'Is that all? Goodbye.' Her hand was already on the door when I exploded.

'Never in my life have I met somebody so rude. Poor Phipps!' With the speed of a top she turned round and looked at me with those huge eyes.

'I am sorry if I have offended you. I did not mean to. I thought you wanted me to look at your things. I am very shy. I cannot talk to people just to make conversation. I hate social life!' Her face suddenly emerged warm and loving. We rushed into the sisterly embrace which sealed our friendship.

From Delhi Stella was going to Jaipur and Ajmer on a government mission. She asked me if I would like to accompany her. Since Maurice was off to East Bengal to assess the needs of the port of Chittagong and could not take me with him I was delighted. It was a unique opportunity to learn about India from one of its most distinguished art experts.

That trip was my first introduction to the real India. I still remember every incident after more than forty years.

In Jaipur we stayed in the Maharajah's guest-house where, as luck would have it, Ram Gopal and his troupe were also staying. They had performed at the Palace the previous day and were leaving next morning. Remembering how much I had enjoyed Ram Gopal's performance in Paris before the war, I asked Stella if she could introduce me to the dancer.

'Introduce you, my dear, but of course. He is an old friend.

I will ask him to dance for us.' Ram Gopal said he would.

The drawing-room having been cleared, we settled on cushions on the floor, leaning against the rolled-back carpet. Stella, wrapped in an ancient Kashmiri shawl, said: 'Taya, you are going to see Bharanatyam as it should be seen and is rarely seen; not on a stage with people sitting in rows at the theatre, but as it used to be performed by dancing girls in the temples when they were entertaining the Gods, in private.'

Ram Gopal's musicians were squatting cross-legged on a rug at one side of the emptied room. Their instruments, with the exception of the drum, were new to me. Most intriguing were two kinds of mandolins separated by a very long and intricate arm. Stella said it was a vina. She was going to explain the difference between the vina and the sithar when Ram Gopal came in, the slow thunder of a hundred little bells attached to his ankles.

Magnificent in shimmering pleated silks, bejewelled, painted - glorious peacock. He stopped in the middle of the room facing us. Hands joined in prayer he bowed from the waist, very low, as if we were his Gods. Swaggering backwards to the thumping of his belled bare feet, he retreated to the wall only to spring forward, noiselessly, without even the littlest shudder of bells. With a nod to the musicians, he began to dance. Stella said that each movement, each gesture, each flutter of hand or brow, had a meaning. The dance was a story. My artistic education had begun.

After three dances Ram Gopal came and sat between us. An ugly little woman had been keeping time slapping her thigh with one hand. Ram Gopal told her to dance.

'Her name is Lakshmi Kantha. She is my guru's daughter and has become my guru. I do not let people watch when she dances. She thinks it's because she has a hare-lip. Her face looks like death. But for you, Professor Kramrisch, only for you, I am making an exception. After you see her, I could never dance before you.'

The woman wound bells round her ankles and began to dance. The way she moved, her control as she throbbed and swayed, orchestrating the music with the bells on her feet, the mastery of her timing as her eyes darted in perfect unison with the drum, the graceful speed with which her neck moved across her shoulders, multiplying her head, erasing the hare-lip, as if by magic. In her South Indian cotton sari, checkered black and ochre, without ornaments, without make-up or flowers, she was truly beautiful. In all my years in India, with the exception of the great Bala Saraswati, I have not seen such sublime dancing. Lakshmi Kantha was *the dance*, like I imagine, Nijinsky. She danced and danced and danced till long after dawn. She would have gone on dancing had it not been time for the train. Ram Gopal and his troupe left without breakfast.

We saw them off, had a bath and our breakfast before going to the Koti Khana, the Maharajah's private treasure House - now a Museum - where the Curator showed us everything. Stella wanted to select works of art to be sent abroad for an exhibition.

It is so long ago that I do not remember what I saw, except that I fell in love with Indian miniatures. Until Jaipur I would have argued that no miniatures in the world could match Fouquet's to which French painting owes so much. In addition to pictures, the Koti Khana had a marvellous collection of rugs and carpets, best of all the Garden Carpet ordered by Aurangzeb. Only a few yards were on show, it had never been used and was still rolled up with pepper, tobacco and neem leaves. At Stella's request it was unrolled. We admired the delicate and colourful floral patterns which made up that huge carpet's mosaic of rectangular gardens. Each one more exquisite than the next.

I was stung with a passion for Indian miniatures. Later, in Delhi, I saw a Moghul painting, a page from the Iskandra Nama - the Book of Alexander - which I had to buy. The artist had shown considerable humour in an attempt to create perpetual motion. Flying above a mountainous landscape with armed horsemen Alexander the Great sat on a platform shaped like a four-poster bed. Harnessed to the top of each poster an eagle flew in eternal pursuit of a chunk of meat tantalisingly out of reach. The asking price, a thousand rupees, was a small fortune we did not have. The dealer agreed to keep the picture for me. In due course, with Stella's blessings, I sold a heavy gold chain which had belonged to my unfavourite grand-mother and bought Alexander's flight to Asia. That picture, one of our most precious possessions, was stolen by the packers fifteen years later when we left India. It was still insured for a thousand rupees.

As Maurice's sister was getting married I took advantage of being in Jaipur to buy her a wedding present. Jaipur has a reputation for precious stones. Stella took me to a jewel-cum-antique shop she knew. Before going in she instructed me to haggle. While I was reducing the price of the double string of carved emeralds which I would have dearly liked for myself, Stella noticed a seventeenth century folk art manuscript of the Ramayana - the story of the God Rama. She was so enthusiastic that the dealer, fearing he had underpriced it, suddenly remembered it was on commission for someone he could not contact. Stella offered twice the original price; he still refused. She was heartbroken.

'I cannot pay more. You know Taya, I have offered him more than three months of my salary at the University. It is not worth more than what he asked at first, but I simply *must* have it for my own collection. I will try again in a couple of months.' Thwarted collector, Stella was prey to withdrawal symptoms.

From the jeweller's shop we wandered to the bazaar. A feast for the senses. Monticules of colourful spices vied with each other and with flowers for scent. Fruit, vegetables, pots, brassware and tinsel, everything. The saleswomen alone deserved the visit. Admirably dressed in short-sleeved embroidered brassieres with a suggestive uplift, bare backs and midriffs the colour of bronze. And, below those glowing skins, the most beautiful skirts in the world. Cut into strips like parachutes, they grew from the waist to twenty-eight yards of folds at the ankles; bell-shaped, billowing with each other. Those Rajputana skirts of coarse hessian, bright green, dark sepia, or black, handblocked with small motifs in red, orange, green or black, are real works of art. The hems, finished with a lining of contrasting colour, transformed those peasants into gigantic flowers swaying in the sun. Stella said I could not buy such a skirt because they were made to order. I gave her no peace until she found a pavement tailor to make me one, complete with choli - the short sleeved brassiere - for thirteen rupees, a bargain at one pound. I chose a dark-brick cloth scattered with small green and orange flowers and a bright green lining. Crowds gathered goggle-eyed to watch the crazy memsahib. Choli and skirt were ready the next day when we came back from Amber. I loved that skirt and wore it in the evening, with the choli or a white chemisier, to the amused scandal of some memsahibs. It took years before my sartorial example was followed by the young Indian nationalist socialites whose predilection for French chiffon over India's gorgeous textiles I never understood.

We climbed Amber by elephant. The last time I had been on an elephant was in the zoo, as a child. This elephant belonged to the Maharajah. Painted all over, with floral garlands of delicate pastel shades, shod with belled anklets like a dancer, jewels round its neck and over its forehead. A splendidly beturbanned mahout sat cross-legged on the animal's neck, in front of the canopied howdah of red velvet and gold braids in which we sat.

Amber towers atop a steep cliff, shimmering in the sunshine, gigantically white and russet gold, mirrored in the lake at its feet. As we approached the fortified palace through a long winding open tunnel hewn in the rock, Stella told me that Amber was some seven hundred years old and had been the capital of the Mina tribe.

'It is named after Amba, the fertility Goddess. There is a lingam in the lake, it is half submerged. The lingam is the symbol of life, it represents the male organ and is most holy.' As she spoke we crossed seven gates before reaching the palace. Everything was elephant scale; getting down did not require a ladder, it was easy as getting off a train. Above the three-tiered entrance gate I noticed the garish statute of a grotesquely fat creature with an elephant head painted bright red, green and gold, dressed in a red sari.

'Stella, is Amber an elephant palace?' She laughed.

'No. This is Ganesh, the God of good fortune. Just to give you an idea of the complexity and morality of Hinduism, let me tell you about Ganesh. Shiva and Parvati, his consort, lived happily together until Shiva decided to wander the world. He left, unaware that Parvati was pregnant. When he returned, years later, unannounced, he flew into a jealous rage at the handsome youth beside his wife and cut off his head before Parvati could stop him. Shattered to learn he had slain his own son he stormed out promising to replace Ganesh's head with that of the first living being he met. That is how Ganesh comes to have an elephant's head. And, since nothing is impossible for the Gods, Ganesh rides a mouse. Contrast that with Shiva not knowing he had a son and notice how he was punished for his jealous behaviour.'

'But what about Ganesh? It was not his fault. He looks grotesque.'

'You and I may think he looks grotesque. Hindus don't. They love him very much. He is their God of good luck to whom they pray when they want to succeed.'

We had entered the palace proper through a series of courtyards. Amber is reputed to be the most impressive of the Rajput fortified palaces. I have visited it at least four times since but, except for that elephant ride, all I remember is Ganesh. I have no problem in his riding a mouse since he is divine, but I continue to find it impossible to reconcile myself to Shiva's behaviour - leaving Parvati for no reason and beheading an innocent. Gods should be more judicious. Stella would argue that Gods are fallible, and should be pitied and forgiven, like humans.

We left Jaipur by the evening train. An overnight journey to Ajmer. In the cosy intimacy of our two berth compartment Stella fell into a reminiscent mood. I forget what made her switch from ballet to Indian Art but I vividly remember her account of the first lecture she gave in London.

'I was terribly nervous. My English was elementary. But Phipps told me not to worry because abstract words in English are borrowed from Latin or Greek. I already knew most of them. When I finished speaking, Sir John Rothenstein got up and thanked me for enriching the English language in the course of a most interesting talk.' Stella laughed at the memory. 'It can't have been too bad. I was offered a lectureship at London University. A godsend because of Hitler. Three years later, when we landed in Bombay I said we had arrived in Bomb A but Indians did not understand. They had not been through the Blitz.'

Taking out a thermos flask, she offered me the coffee she had brought from Jaipur. 'Remember, my dear, never, but *never* under any circumstances eat or drink something which has not been boiled or thoroughly disinfected. That is the only way to avoid getting dysentery or worse. Never eat a salad you have not yourself supervised being cleaned or rinsed in a solution of potassium pemanganate. Never eat fruits which have been peeled or cut by somebody else, never eat from a cold buffet, except yoghurt, always remember that flies contaminate food. If the food is piping hot it is quite safe.' Good advice. Very often, when I failed to follow it, I got dysentery.

'Have I told you that we are the guests of Sir Bagchand Soni. He is a leading citizen of Ajmer and very rich. His hobby is collecting jewels. He is a very orthodox Jain. Jains are a Hindu sect which follows Mahavira, an ascetic prince contemporary of the Buddha, but much more rigorous in his teachings. Jains are forbidden to take life. Their monks and nuns cover their mouths and noses with cloth to stop them swallowing flying insects and they sweep the ground in front of their feet not to tread on small creatures like ants. They don't eat root vegetables, only things which fall off, like fruit or seeds. Feeding vermin is a way they have of acquiring merit. There are rich Jains who pay paupers to lie on beds ridden with bed-bugs so that the bed-bugs can gorge themselves. Sir Bagchand Soni feeds crows every day. And I know another rich businessman who feeds pie-dogs. Sir Bagchand Soni is far too orthodox to let us into his house. We would pollute it; he has a lovely guest-house. He does not know that you are coming but Indian hospitality is fantastic It will give him an opportunity to show off his emeralds.'

Very tall, bulky, immaculate in a knee-length dazzling white ajkhan with six diamond buttons, each the size of a rupee, Sir Bagchand Soni was waiting on the platform.

'Welcome, my dear Professor, welcome . . . Of course I know Maurice Zinkin. Dear lady, I have had dealings with your husband when he was in Textile Control. It will be an honour, as well as a pleasure, to have you stay in my humble home.' He took us to the guest-house, left us to unpack and bathe. Train journeys in India can be exceedingly dusty and sooty.

Overlooking the town, his guest-house was very different from Jaipur's, which is now a tourist hotel. Sir Bagchand Soni's guest-house was a luxurious villa, comfortable and characterless. Four double bedroomed suites, complete with mosquito-nets, ceiling-fans, dressing-rooms and bathrooms, opened into a large drawing-room where, unobtrusively set into the wall, a safe had been provided for guests' valuables. The dining-room, like the drawing-room, was furnished with a cross between PWD and Art Deco. Massively comfortable furniture, casual tables with chiselled brass trays, silver cigarette cases, alabaster ashtrays, jejune watercolour pictures of English hollyhocked cottages. Large persian carpets on polished marble floors and spectacular floral arrangements in alabaster urns lent colour to a monochrome background.

Breakfast, except for the fruit, was insipid. No life had been sacrificed on our account.

'His food is awful because he is such a strict vegetarian,' Stella said, adding that, as predicted, I was most welcome. 'These guest-houses are there for people like us and of course for family overspills. Some foreigners exploit Indian hospitality shamelessly. All one needs is one letter of introduction, preferably to a Maharajah who will pass you on to another. There are enough Maharajahs to last years, especially if one does the rounds again.' Stella nearly choked with laughter on a banana. 'I can still see her. I was getting off the train in Mysore when a convoy of porters from the Palace arrived carrying an elderly European woman on a string cot. She was in her housecoat. They dumped her and her paraphernalia in the train. The ADC who was meeting me said she had arrived two years earlier with an introduction from the Nizam and was being forcibly sent on to the Maharani of Travancore.' Stella had barely finished her story when Sir Bagchand Soni came to say his car was at our disposal. We drove to the Museum.

The whole world now knows about the glory of Hindu Art but for me in 1946 it was a revelation. I had never seen any. In Delhi the art was magnificent but Muslim. The Museum was crammed to overflowing with statues mostly of the Gupta period which Stella said was one of the best. Dirty, clumsily numbered with indelible ink, covered with dusty cobwebs, peppered with mice and bat droppings, stacked pell-mell, those statues throbbed with life. The plasticity, the tender voluptuousness of those bodies entwined in love shone through the grime of neglect. I could have sworn they breathed. Faces, too, were alive, passionate or enigmatic like that wistful Parvati whose smile fleeted like Mona Lisa's. I was lost in contemplation. Stella was selecting. This done she dusted off her skirt and instructed the Curator with the methodical elementary thoroughness teachers reserve for children.

'Remember, I don't want *anything* to happen in transit. Those statues have to travel thousands of miles by train, boat and truck. I have explained to you how they should be packed. If they have suffered by the time they arrive in England you will be personally responsible.' In the car she said the Museum was typical of India's lack of concern for the national heritage. Now, of course, it is different.

From the Museum we drove to Pushkar Lake to watch the sunset. That lake is almost as sacred as the Ganges. Pilgrims were busy on stone slabs by the water's edge. Some were lost in contemplative prayer. One old man stood frozen in a yogic headstand. A couple of women soaped clothes. A youth, astride a half-submerged water buffalo, was giving it a scrub. Heads and shoulders appeared, engaged in ritual ablutions within a stone's throw of a couple of large crocodiles.

'It is most unusual for people to be eaten,' Stella assured me.

On return to the guest-house it was decided that I had better stay in Ajmer where there was a great deal more to see, while Stella went to inspect a site in the jungle, a day's jeep-drive away. When I woke up she had already left.

After breakfast Lady Soni came to see me. She did not stay long, half an hour perhaps. There was a purpose to her visit. Wrapped in an oyster-pink French chiffon sari modestly pulled over her head, she looked like an ageing Murillo Madonna. Finely cut features, big luminous black eyes, perfect eyebrows. She wore little jewelry. Everything about her was subdued, gentle, faintly sad. Her English was excellent. After enquiring about my comfort she spoke affectionately of her youngest son who was reaching boarding-school age. She hoped to persuade her husband to choose the Doon School rather than Scindia or the Mayo College for Maharajahs. Did I agree with her? She was pleased I did.

'I wish you would say that to Himself. He will listen to you more than to me, you are so much better educated.' Before I could protest she added with a deep blush that Himself had told her I was a doctor. Stella had mentioned I only had to get my degree and I had not corrected her in front of our host. Lady Soni blushed even more deeply. She must have had a very fair skin for I do not recollect Indians blushing. It was then I realised she had come for medical advice from a woman doctor. Women doctors in India were mostly missionaries.

'I am not quite a doctor yet, but is there something I can do for you?' There was. She wanted advice on contraception. From Delhi I sent her a supply of foam tablets called Volpar, after Voluntary Parenthood. 'Please don't tell Himself. Let this be our little secret.'

I spent the best part of that day strolling about Ajmer. There was much to see. Most impressive were the ruins of the Adhai Mosque with its massive screen of fretted stone and its many columns, each one differently carved. And there was the tomb of a Muslim saintly ascetic with heavy silver doors and two attached mosques. Most of all I enjoyed watching silversmiths pound tiny squares of silver and gold into wafer thin sheets, so thin that they stuck to everything. In India, those flimsy precious wafers are used to decorate food.

Sir Bagchand Soni was waiting for me in the drawing-room. By his side, on the sofa, there were two large flat leather jewel cases.

'I thought you might like to see my necklaces.'

'Stella tells me your emeralds are famous all over India. I would love to see them.'

What a sight! Thirteen rows of flawless dark green stones, the centre ones as big as walnuts. Enough to cover an entire chest with a glittering armour. The gigantic clasp from Cartier was splendid. In the other case there was a similar necklace, but of pearls.

'When Lady Willingdon came to Ajmer I was foolish enough to wear my pearls in her honour. I did not know that the Vicereine collects pearls. As you can see, there are only twelve strings now. I was lucky to get away with giving her the smallest.'

Sir Bagchand insisted on putting the emeralds, which he said were insured for two and a quarter million pounds, on my neck. 'Look in the mirror. They match your eyes.' When I tried to take them off he suggested I wear them for a while. He would return soon and dashed off before I could stop him.

I had been put in an intolerable position. A position made the more intolerable because Maurice's King Emperor would expect me to handle it with tact.

I locked the emeralds in the safe. Like Sister Anne, I began to look for salvation. It was then I spotted two servants carrying a large basket filled with mouthwatering pancakes for the crows. I helped myself shamelessly to a couple and followed them to the flat roof to watch the feast. From the roof I could see the hills, and the Civil Lines. Enquiry revealed that the nearest house was that of the Chief Engineer of the Railway. The servants added that Moore Memsahib was a great shikari. I walked as fast as I could to that bungalow and found Mrs Moore on the verandah. I explained my predicament. She sent a servant to collect my things and deliver a letter to Lady Soni saying that, as we were old friends, she insisted on my staying with her until Stella's return.

At first I thought I had misunderstood the servants when they said Mrs Moore was a great shikari, a famous huntress. Middle-aged, tiny, long curls bunched above her ears like Goldilocks', she had been busy painting. Postcards were drying on a trestle table: wreaths of forget-me-nots with a central heart, honeysuckled thatched cottages, hollyhocks by gates bearing 'Welcome' signs.

'Watercolouring is a profitable hobby', she explained over tea and home-baked cakes. 'I also paint pictures. Sir Bagchand has bought quite a few.'

She was a hunter all right. Far more impressive than the trophies in her bungalow was her photographic album. There was a picture of two enormous bears. 'I really got scared that time. We had been stalking one bear, not realising there was another. When I shot it, its mate rushed out and had to be killed at point-blank range. It nearly fell on me.' By 'we' she meant herself and her small dachshund bitch. 'The best-hunting dog in the whole world.' Except for that dog, scaled down to her own size, Mrs Moore always hunted alone leaving the servants with the tents. 'Shooting from elephants is cheating. And beaters are more of a nuisance than anything.'

Bear and tiger shooting were her speciality. She had earned many rewards for killing man-eaters. What she enjoyed most was getting ibex.

'To find an ibex and get near enough without being spotted is far more challenging than stalking a wounded tiger. Ibex are as swift as lightning and, at fourteen to eighteen thousand feet, the mountain is on their side.'

13

Princes and prima donnas

The next time I went to Rajasthan was as the guest of the Diwan - Prime Minister of Bikaner. A shared passion for History had brought Sardar Panikkar and Maurice together before our marriage. My being French, and a shared devotion to Proust, sealed our friendship. The Prime Minister of Bikaner hankered with rosied nostalgia after the Paris of his youth.

A seventeen-gun salute Princely State, two thirds the size of Scotland, Bikaner owed everything to Maharajah Ganga Singh, Panikkar's late master and hero.

'He was a lion among men. And so far-sighted. So patriotic. When Ganga Singh was only eighteen years old a terrible famine struck Bikaner. Many people died. There was nothing he could do. The State was a backward sandy desert fit only for camels. You should see, Taya, *ma chère amie,* our famous Camel Corps. In those early days, the camel was the main mode of locomotion - 1898 you know. After he toured the disaster area on camel-back Ganga Singh swore by the sun and the moon, his ancestors, that such a calamity would never happen again. By the late twenties the Ganga Canal had turned one thousand square miles of desert into a granary. Mind you, it can't have been easy. There's no water in Bikaner. But Ganga Singh did not rest until the Viceroy, and the King who was his friend, allowed him to tap the Sutlej river. It is also thanks to him that there is a railway. HH was also obsessed with the need to transport supplies quickly. You will never guess his last words. 'Bring me the Bhakra Dam file.' That file, my dear lady, is about a Government of India project to build a gigantic dam in the Punjab.

'What a great man we lost! In some ways he was like Louis Quatorze. To be present at his levée was an honour and quite a to-do. Before his bath the ADC in charge of his wardrobe led a procession of bearers carrying some fifty suits for him to choose from. A drawer full of detachable collars would follow, with an army of shirts and one hundred ties on a rack. There were matching pochettes and socks, of course, and then, on a velvet tray, cuff-links and studs. He took his bath while the clothes he had chosen were brushed and ironed. When he came out of the bath, all scented, his moustache was neatly pressed in a fine hair-net caught at the ears. He was very particular about his moustache. A perfectionist in everything. A great believer in never wasting a single minute, while dressing he dictated to his stenographer. His WC was equipped so that he could write letters. A great believer, too, in keeping records he used to insist that all of us carry notebooks wherever we went. "Don't trust your brains, write it down," he kept nagging. There was nothing he liked better than work. Sometimes he started, and I would have to start also, at four o' clock in the morning and went on till perhaps ten o' clock at night. A lion I tell you.'

In the 30's Panikkar had been Foreign Minister to the Maharajah of Patiala.

'His Highness Patiala was irrepressible.' Panikkar's face lit up at the memory while nervous fingers kept stroking the goatee he cherished under the illusion it increased his resemblance to Lenin.

'One of my jobs as Foreign Minister was to accompany HH abroad to try and keep his spending within the limits of his lavish privy purse. A thankless task if ever there was one! I remember the time, in Paris, he gave me the slip. Fortunately I had an arrangement with the chauffeur. So I went to Cartier and cancelled an order for six dozen diamond and gold ladies' wrist-watches. I had quite a job convincing the manager. Back in Patiala, there were so many jewels still unpacked from previous jaunts to Europe that HH never noticed that the watches had not been sent.'

'Why six dozen ladies' wrist watches?'

'My dear Taya, you may well ask. Why six dozen and not thirty dozen? HH always bought in bulk. He had no less than three hundred concubines, not to mention his lawful wives. You know, Sawa Singh Gill, that enormous Sikh, the one you told me was so fat and heavy that you saw the horse go up in the air, like on a seesaw, when he boarded a tonga at the Club, well his brother is a Patiala official who enjoys the title of "Keeper of the Conscience of His Highness." His job is to look after the Lalbag Palace where the concubines and their childen are kept. Fortunately for the State, HH could be very mean towards concubines, some times giving them paste instead of the real thing.

'But let me give you an idea of the way he did his shopping. When the representative from Rankens called he would order one hundred shirts at a time and, if he was in a good mood, half a dozen suits for me. He was extravagant. You will be amused to know that he suddenly got it into his head that the concubines must be modern and wear pyjamas with sailor tops. All three hundred of them, except those visibly in the family way. I still remember the sight! It was in Simla. HH walking the Mall, followed at a respectful distance by the French Merchant Navy: navy blue and white, bell-shaped, complete except for the red pompoms.'

Such of Panikkar's time not spent attempting to restrain his master's extravagance went on fruitless representations to the Viceroy in order to establish Patiala's ranking ahead of Bikaner. A bulky file, stretching over half a dozen years eloquently testified to the importance Indian Princes attached to precedence. Panikkar chuckled.

'An exasperated official of the Political Department noted on that file:

'The Viceroy is getting very tired of the petty difficulties that arise over precedence.' Bikaner had the edge over Patiala from the very start as I kept reminding HH. For one thing he had been the only Princely Member of the Imperial War Cabinet during the First World War. For another, he was an intimate friend of the King. He had been his ADC before the King's marriage. I could not tell HH that, in addition, the British were not impressed by the number of his concubines or his spending sprees - be it the hiring of the entire floor of the Ritz or buying up the contents of a music shop in Vienna because he had forgotten the name of the score his conductor asked him to bring back. No. Patiala did not stand a chance against Bikaner, just as Nabha did not stand a chance against Patiala.'

As usual, Panikkar had been talking non-stop that evening. Admirable raconteur, I could listen to him all night. After dinner we selected a table in the penumbra of the Club terrace.

'Did you say Nabha did not stand a chance against Patiala, but over what? Surely so small a State could not rank higher?'

'It was not over gun-salutes, but over a woman.' Panikkar's face suddenly sprang closer to mine, sensuous, Machiavellian. Waving his long cigarette holder he warned: '*My dear lady*, always remember that it was the great Marcel who insisted that life is stranger than fiction. How right he was! I am going to tell you a story which, unbelievable as it sounds, is absolutely true and goes something like a nasty fairy tale.' After that introduction he told me an incredible story of which I was reminded, in the late fifties, by an obituary notice in the local press.

In a Patiala village lived a pretty peasant girl. She was married to a sepoy of the Indian Army and went, with her husband, to the Far East where he became batman to a British Officer. The Officer seduced her. The batman murdered his Officer, was court-martialled and executed. The widow was sent back to India on a troop-ship. During the voyage two NCOs fought over her, killing each other. Back in her husband's village, the widow was seen by a British Deputy Inspector General of Police who made her his concubine. For this breach of convention he was demoted, transferred and forbidden to see her again. Shortly after that, the Maharajah of Nabha, out on a duck shoot, straying into Patiala saw her, had her abducted and brought to his Palace. The Maharajah of Patiala, having by then heard of her beauty, sent for her. Learning she had been kidnapped he protested to his fellow ruler demanding her return. Nabha married her instead and, afraid of what Patiala might do, had her walled into a room of his Palace where nobody could get at her. Food was brought through a small hatch. Then Nabha officially complained to the Viceroy that Patiala had kidnapped one of his wives. This was a serious allegation which the Viceroy could not ignore. An enquiry was set up.

'HH was asked to explain. Fortunately our spies had discovered the truth and we were able to provide the Viceroy with the facts, including a sketch of the place where the woman was kept. Nabha was deposed and the woman was sent back to her village with an annuity from the Political Department. She is still there, alone. And will you believe it, *chère amie*, at the time her saga ends she was only sixteen.'

'She must be incredibly beautiful. Have you seen her?'

'No. Like HH, I was scared. She brings the evil eye.'

Until I came to India, had I been asked to name Maharajahs, I would, like many French people, have said 'Kapurthala' and stopped.

Kapurthala was well-known in Paris. As a child I used to pass his luxurious residence on my way to the Bois. India's Croesus was notorious for the lavishness of his parties.

On one occasion, to amuse his wife, he told a distinguished, hand-picked gathering, that finders would keep the precious stones hidden in the drawing-room. A friend of my parents' described the ensuing pandemonium which proved that civilisation was not even skin-deep. Guests clawed at the furniture, ripped carpets and curtains, fought like animals.

However, Kapurthala's popularity was grounded not in eccentricity but in a deep-seated Francophilia of which I was reminded by one of Panikkar's letters:

> 'My Dear Taya,
>
> This is a fantastic little France I have been living in. The palace is a replica of Versailles. All the furniture is Louis Quinze. Two rooms are Empire style. The drawing-room with its gilt ceilings and French mural paintings of the seasons (represented by naked but beautiful women), with all the decorations in the best French taste create such a fantastic atmosphere. We dine off Royal Blue Sèvres, drink French white wine (of the supremest quality) at lunch and champagne at dinner. The cooking is by French chefs from Paris! HH speaks to his family in French.
>
> It is a kind of vanished Bourbon Court which has suddenly come into existence and HH who is 77 years old still goes through the strenuous life of a fashionable potentate. At a garden party yesterday he was announced with a fanfare of trumpeters. You should come here if you want to see what the Court of the Smaller Bourbons was like in the 17th century.
>
> With love,
>
> KMP

I never went to Kapurthala but I did go to Bikaner. Panikkar had invited us because he wanted Maurice to persuade the Maharajah to accept his Budget proposals. HH Sadul Singh was not like his august father. Matters of State left him indifferent. His Prime Minister was banking on my husband's eloquence.

We were met at the station by a Secretary who explained that the Prime Minister was detained at the Palace.

'Mrs Panikkar is expecting you for tea. But I must warn you. She does not speak English or Hindi, only Malayalam.' Malayalam, the language of Kerala, Panikkar's native State, is different from other Indian languages.

Small, dark, grey-hair-in-a-small-bun, our hostess sat at a table on the terrace. Remembering Panikkar's affection for cherry brandy, we had brought a bottle and gave it to his wife. With a broad grin she nodded her thanks and said something to the bearer who came back with three high-ball glasses and opened the bottle. We declined. Mrs Panikkar poured herself a sizeable helping. Maurice whispered in dismay.

'This is *terrible*. Orthodox ladies do not drink. It will go to her head. We must do something.' I said loudly, pointing to the bottle: 'It is for Sardar Panikkar.' I said it in English and in Urdu. In English I added that it contained alcohol. Mrs Panikkar did not understand. She kept smiling. Short of snatching the glass from her hand there was nothing we could do. She obviously liked the sweet taste and poured herself a second, and larger, helping which she drank in sips interspersed with appreciative smacks of the tongue against her lips. I tried to remove the bottle. She held on to it. We sat, petrified as she went through a third helping. By the time Panikkar arrived the bottle was half-empty. His wife, somewhat flushed, was stone sober.

'Isn't she fantastic! She says it's better than sherbet. But my dear friends, let me wish you the warmest welcome, even if you are turning my wife into an alcoholic.'

It was interesting to see Panikkar at home. The man of the world, the skilled politician, the historian who should have remained an academic, was visibly afraid of his wife. Maurice later explained that this was true of many Indians and that Panikkar's caste, the Nairs, are matriarchal.

Mrs Panikkar had enjoyed the cherry brandy so much that, discarding caste taboos, she let me watch her in the kitchen while our husbands talked shop. Watching her chop vegetables was even more fascinating than watching her drink. She installed herself on the floor, grabbed a sharp instrument and held it firmly between her heels, the cutting edge pointing towards her. Holding the vegetables in both hands she pressed them against the chopper. With both hands free it is much easier to cut or chop.

That evening we dined at the Palace, *dans l'intimité*, just the four of us. Mrs Panikkar had been asked but did not accept.

'You tell your master I do not see why I should expose myself to his eyes when he keeps his wife in purdah. Go tell him this is what I said.' Panikkar was upset. 'My wife is adamant. I had hoped that, with just the two of you and His Highness, she would make an exception. It is most embarrassing for me. As you know, a Ruler's invitation is a Command. When I was in Patiala she stayed in Travancore but when I came to Bikaner she insisted on coming with me. What makes it worse is that I can't even pretend she is in purdah. She goes wherever she pleases. Nair ladies are very emancipated. We Nair men are just drones.'

What I remember from that meal - the food was British non-descript - is the impressive collection of hunting trophies in the Great Hall. A famous hunter of big game, HH had, as the trophies proclaimed, also roamed Africa. The water colours in the small room where we ate, bore such a striking resemblance to Mrs Moore's handiwork that I asked if he knew her. At the mention of her name HH's face lit up. For the first two courses, he waxed eloquent on a subject so dear to his heart that all Panikkar's attempts to broach the Budget fell on an ear deaf by design. Having killed countless beasts, he now only shot them with a cine-camera. Would I like to see some of the African films?' Gently kicked under the table by Panikkar, I declined, pleading a slight headache.

Panikkar got his way in the end. Maurice talked finance, a subject HH found as boring as it enthralled Maurice. Over coffee, having listened to enough facts, figures and tax proposals, he interrupted Maurice to ask if I had seen 'Trader Horn'. I had and shared his admiration. If I remember right, the Maharajah of Bikaner had actually been on location during some of the animal sequences. Before leaving we were invited by HH to come back for the Imperial Sand Grouse Shoot.

On the way back to his house Panikkar complained bitterly.

'What would the Great Ganga Singh have said! To prefer cinema to matters of State! Your French charm obviously worked on His Highness. Actually, I am delighted he invited you. That way Maurice will have another chance to educate him. And I am sure you will enjoy the week-end enormously. It's quite an event you know. An experience not to be missed. But, to think that HH had an opportunity to pick Maurice's brain - a brain, if you don't mind my saying so of the very best, and I am not exaggerating - and to discuss 'Trader Horn' instead! And then they say that if things go well one must praise the Ruler but that if they go wrong it is the fault of the Prime Minister! What am I to do? I have no magic wand. I am my master's servant! Did you notice, *chère amie*, the way HH kept looking at his watch. It's barely eleven o'clock but he was in a hurry to go to his mistress.'

'Some dancing girl?' Maurice asked.

'*Pas du tout*. On the contrary, a society lady. The wife of a senior Railway Officer. You will meet her. A very lively lady from Bengal. Well connected with a husband either blind or accommodating. It is a pretty public affair.' Panikkar burst out laughing. 'His father was much more circumspect. As you know, he was intimate with King George. Well, after HH died I had to go through his papers. There was a whole file with letters from the King to his friend. The letters were personal, often written late in the evening after his Majesty had had a few drinks. It was quite extraordinary. Those letters were dotted with numbered cut-out bits. The numbers had been methodically pasted in where words were missing. In a separate file I found the missing words, also carefully numbered. Will you believe it! HH had censored all the expletives and the swear words, but kept them for reference.'

Shared admiration for Mrs Moore and 'Trader Horn' having produced that invitation to the Imperial Sand Grouse Shoot, I witnessed one of the most prestigious carnages in the world.

Like the other guests, we arrived by special train, in good time to change for drinks before dinner. In sharp contrast to the informality of our previous encounter this was a grand affair.

As I had not eaten off gold before, I tried - without success - to discover whether that precious metal, credited with medicinal as well as erotic properties, affected the taste. I sat between General Sir Rob Lockhart - he succeeded Auchinleck as Commander in Chief of independent India - and a distinguished physician from Berlin imported by the late Maharajah to run his hospital. The doctor and I became friends there and then. Facing us sat the delightful teenage daughter of the GOC Northern Command, General Sir Frank Masservy, a debutante, fresh out from England for the winter season. Her name, I seem to remember, was Rosemary . . . or should have been. She looked so much like a bud.

Women at this banquet were few. The Generals' wives,

Rosemary, the Hospital Matron, the wife of the Manager of the Railways, a handsome lady in a brocade sari glistening with gold and jewelry, and myself. The Maharani, being in purdah, was absent, so were Mrs Panikkar and the lady with whom the doctor was living.

Besides the massive gold plates what I best remember from that evening is Rosemary's wide-eyed enjoyment and the double standard which kept the doctor's companion away. HH's mistress was present because her husband chaperoned her. The doctor's companion was absent although the only reason they were not married was that she was waiting for a divorce from the adventurer she had married to escape from Nazi Germany.

Shortly after that dinner we were driven to the Gajner shooting-lodge, a small modern palace some distance from town. Bed-tea and a collation appeared at five o'clock the next morning. Warmly dressed, we were posted in threes in rows of butts overlooking a lake. There we waited, each one of us equipped with a small hip-flask of brandy and a loader with two guns. It was so cold that the brandy was most welcome. Suddenly a dark cloud appeared on the horizon. The sand-grouse were flying in to drink. The Maharajah's opening shot shattered the silence. Soon I was reminded of that time during the war when, fleeing the German advance, I was straffed by low-flying planes. Only now the shooting was upwards and I was safe in my butt, protected from the feathered downpour. Can there be skill in carnage of such magnitude? The birds were so thick in the air that aiming seemed unnecessary. Within a couple of hours three thousand sand-grouse had been murdered.

After lunch we were treated to a jeep-ride through open country and we raced a herd of black-buck, bouncing ping-pong-like creatures who kept leaping joyfully in every direction, safe in the knowledge that theirs was protected territory.

'The Great Lady has arrived! I will take you to her for darshan - blessing.' Panikkar who had taken my political education in hand sounded most excited over the telephone.

He arrived, splendid in beige. Edwardian down to his gaiters and the flowing pochette matching the tie stabbed into place by a jewelled pin. Nicotine and leucoderma-stained, manicured fingers kept teasing his goatee. Deep-set eyes sparkling as he bombarded me with information.

'Sarojini Naidu, our great poetess, the Nightingale of India, is a woman in a million! No, not in a million, in a crore (ten million). You may not think so when you meet her but she has been a great beauty. She and Jinnah were madly in love with each other once; he was still in the Congress then. She is a Queen. Such wit, such charm. Such charisma. Such style. You will simply adore her . . . we all do. She is a force of nature. But let's go.

I already knew that Mrs Naidu was a great supporter of the Congress. She had accompanied Gandhi to the Round Table Conference and had told the British press that it cost a fortune to keep the Mahatma in poverty. I had met one of her daughters - a tall, skinny blue-stocking.

'So you know Padmaja! She tries to copy her mother, down to those gorgeous saris and the heavy make-up.'

'You must be joking, Huzur (Your Honour, my nickname for my friend). She does not dress up and looks like a boy. There's nothing gorgeous about her.'

Panikkar burst out laughing. 'My mistake, *ma chère*. So it was Leelamani you met, not Padamaja. Leelamani is not a bit like her mother. Probably a thorn in the great lady's flesh, like her son the doctor. If you ever go to Hyderabad, be sure to call on him. Delightful fellow, most civilized. A real gentleman and so gentle that it seems incredible he should have wanted to join the Communist Party when he was a student in Germany. You know how Germanic the Germans are. To join their Communist Party one had to present and defend a thesis, just like a degree. Poor fellow, he tried to prove that the next country to go Communist would be China. Such heresy could not be tolerated. Marx postulated that it is the industrialised countries which are ripe for Communism. Now he lives quietly in Hyderabad, practising homoeopathy and waiting for history to prove him right. I expect he does not approve his mother's life style. But enough gossip. I took the liberty of telling the great lady that I was bringing her a chela (disciple). After good food, there is nothing our nightingale likes more than being a guru.'

In Delhi Mrs Naidu stayed with Sir Sri Ram, a textile magnate who put a wing of his mansion at her disposal.

From the cushioned couch upon which she was majestically spread Mrs Naidu was holding court. Draped in the shimmering opulence of a thick taffeta sari, shot purple and burgundy, generously edged in brocade of gold. No hint of Gandhian austerity. Small, squat, fat and flabby with puffed eye-sockets, dark skinned. Yet according to Panikkar she had been a great beauty! Heavily scented and made up, Indian style, with kohl around the eyes and red kumkum above her strong nose, she reminded me of Racine's Athalie: superbly adorned to repair time's irreparable outrage. The way Panikkar behaved in her presence she might have been the Empress Victoria. In a matter of minutes I, too, succumbed to her spell.

She was in Delhi to see doctors about her high blood-pressure and complained they wanted to starve her. 'Sadar, I will come to your dinner but only on condition that we start with paté de fois gras followed by duck à l'orange, chocolate soufflé and plenty of champagne. One only lives once. To hell with dieting! Bad enough that here the kitchens are strictly vegetarian. Probably good for the blood-pressure; but when I go out I want to enjoy myself. Say what you like but the nightingale is ravenous for duck.'

The dinner Panikkar gave in her honour at the Imperial Hotel caused her blood-pressure to shoot up high enough for her doctors to confine her to bed for the fortnight during which I became a regular visitor. She was such fun, so mischievously naughty, so stimulating. I had to tell her what I was doing and she took an impish delight in debunking the people I praised. Her gossip could be most instructive.

I complained that a handsome white-haired man called Sayed Hussein had been very rude to me at a dinner party.

'That gigolo must have been drunk as usual,' and she went on to argue that if Pakistan came into being it would be, to some extent, because of Sayed Hussein.

'History, my child, is often created by quirks; silly quirks of fate. Sayed Hussein was Motilal Nehru's private secretary. Motilal loved him like a son. Sayed used to be part of the household. He and Nan fell in love. Prevented from marrying, they eloped. Nan was eventually brought back. The scandal was hushed up and she married Pandit, a man much older. Sayed was given a lot of money to stay away from India. This is his first visit after many years. It was Mahatma who made it possible for Motilal to allow his daughter to marry a Muslim. Gandhiji said the boy had to become a Hindu first. That's not possible - even in case you don't know, Hindus are born not made. We have no conversion - except to Untouchability. Unfortunately, after Jinnah left the Congress, this gave him extra ammunition for Pakistan. Poor Vijayalaksmi. She was very much in love. I grant you he is good-looking, even now. But he is a drunkard, a woman-chaser, a scoundrel. No self-respecting man would give up the woman he loves for money. She is much better off without him. But enough gossip. Have a mango - the little green ones come from Benares and are delicious.'

Ample supplies of goodies kept converging at Sarojini's court. Saris, shawls, fruit by the basketful. In fairness, her visitors were most welcome to the perishable tokens of her popularity. One day, when I complained that life in India was expensive and that we were finding it difficult to make ends meet, she gave me a stern lecture. The British, she said, were jolly lucky to be in India where they led a life of luxury at the people's expense. It came ill from a Civil Servant's wife to complain, especially since life in India was dirt cheap.

'Dirt cheap for you perhaps, not for me. How much did you pay for those mangoes? And that sari? And those pretty slippers embroidered with seed pearls? And the food, not to mention all the chocolates the doctors say you should not eat? Do you pay for the stamps when you write a letter?'

'All right, my dear! You win. I was naughty!'

I never forgot that verbal fencing. Indians are schizophrenic about honesty. They have a real and profound horror of corruption. Nothing does a man more good than a reputation for total honesty. Our dear friend, A D Gorwala, used to be held up to admiration in the Service, not because he had never taken bribes, but because he had never even been offered one.

The extent to which honesty was valued in India is illustrated by a story Maurice was told by Sir Purshottamdas Thakurdas, Bombay's leading businessman. A certain official was posted to Jamnagar. The Maharajah was the great Ranji, the cricketer. He sent his carriage to the station to meet the Political Agent. The Political Agent sent the carriage back and hired a tonga. The Maharajah was impressed. Sir Purshottamdas still found the story worth telling after thirty years.

Corruption was an Indian obsession. Sex was not. A woman could travel freely alone anywhere in the India of those days. What happened to me in the Dominican Republic during the war was inconceivable in India.

When we landed in Ciudad Trujillo my parents' valuables were kept in bond by the customs and I was photographed. Three months later the Chief of Police called with an official invitation to a cocktail party. He drove me to a country house where Hector Trujillo, the Dictator's brother, in full military uniform, was entertaining a mixed bag: University professors, a couple of doctors, and some women. Before I realised how it happened, he manoeuvred me into a bedroom, locked the door and made crude advances.

'You are so much prettier than your photo. I saw you in the street the other day.' He unbuckled the holster to remove his trousers. Grabbing his revolver I threatened to shoot at the ceiling if he did not let me go.

The second occasion was more serious. The Haitian Ambassador, a friend of my parents, had invited me to a Red Cross Ball attended by the Dictator himself. I was invited to dance with him. Trujillo and I whirled in the centre of a small circle made by the backs of his armed bodyguards who stood facing outwards, hands at the ready on their holsters. After three dances I was returned to the table of the Ambassador who advised me not to go home. I spent the night at the Embassy. Next morning I was smuggled out of Santo Domingo in the car taking the son of President Lescot back to Haiti at the end of an official visit. At the border, I had to lie on the floor, covered by a rug. The Chief of Police, unable to bring me to his master, informed my parents that their valuables would only be returned in exchange for me. I remained in Haiti for six months until we received our emigration visas to America. As soon as these arrived the American Consul demanded the return of my parents' assets and warned the Dominican authorities that I should be left alone. We had become potential American citizens and were at last under Uncle Sam's protection.

14

Mother in India

Mine was not an easy pregnancy. On a good day I kept down my third breakfast, the one meal which carried me through. On a bad day . . . There was that Sunday afternoon when the Civil Surgeon suggested, as I was vomiting blood, that abortion was indicated.

I used to walk Maurice to the Secretariat, for exercise. Often my red-faced husband pretended to ignore the woman retching into the ornamental pools along the way. In Simla, I used to fetch him from work. Maurice's office was on the first floor of a ramshakle building devoid of ladies' loos. I used a small wooden balcony instead. Once a poor old man sleeping underneath was woken up by that unseasonal shower, and was then vomited upon as I retched over the balustrade.

From Simla we went to Ziarat. I was no longer sick by then but I was huge and when I developed a molar abscess, Colonel Ledgard refused to pull the tooth out in case I haemorrhaged. The Colonel, Robin our host, and Maurice took turns to stand on the road to wait for a car on its way down from the Afghan border. Eventually an army truck stopped. It was full but the driver agreed to take me to Quetta's Military Hospital which we reached after midnight. I was rushed to the operating theatre and given a whiff of chloroform. It took so long to extract the tooth that I was fully awake when the doctor broke my jaw. He was not a dentist and it was an emergency. Instead of the morphine he prescribed I was given aspirin. When I complained in the morning the doctor apologised saying the nurse must have sold the morphine in the bazaar. A taxi took me back to Ziarat and I kept seeing imaginary camels on the way.

At the end of Maurice's leave we left Ziarat for Delhi. At Rohri Junction the air-conditioned Karachi-Lahore train was hours late so we lay on the platform. A pie-dog licked Maurice's face. When the train did arrive it had no air-conditioned carriages. We managed to get a tin-tub filled with blocks of ice. 120 degrees in the shade was normal in Sind at that time of year. After I fainted twice I sat on the ice.

We had been absent from Delhi for four months. Our belongings had been shifted to the verandah of our new quarters: a self-contained unit at the end of a drive, some hundred yards from the Club buildings. It was so hot that I kept postponing unpacking to stay in the pool.

We had not been in Delhi a week when Maurice developed diphtheria, probably due to the dog's licking. The Civil Surgeon put him in isolation and rang Mrs Faulder, the Club Secretary. On my return from the hospital I was notified to vacate the premises within 24 hours. Mrs Faulder wanted to fumigate our quarters. I failed to find anywhere to stay. The hotels were full. None of my friends was in Delhi at the time and those of Maurice's colleagues who lived in houses refused to put me up on the ground that their wives were in Simla.

By eight o'clock the next evening I begged Mrs Faulder to let me stay. Accompanied by coolies, she evicted me, dumping everything on the road by the Club's side entrance.

'Even if you are not a carrier and if you keep to your quarters, you have to go because, given your worries, you could give birth any moment and Club rules are formal: children not allowed.' Before coming to Delhi Mrs Faulder had been a missionary in China.

I was sitting on a trunk, surrounded by luggage, stunned. A man in dinner jacket enquired about Zinkin. Back in Simla, Maurice had invited him to dinner. Old enough to be my father, Mr Davey, a senior Civil Aviation official offered me his bed for the night so long as I did not mind his wife being in Simla and our sharing the bathroom.

My guardian angel was staying at 1 Man Singh Road, a private hostel run by Mr Fonseca, a middle-aged Goan with a big heart. The next morning my host, who had spent the night on a couch, asked Mr Fonseca to give me a room, no matter how small. Delhi was so full that Mr Fonseca, his housekeeper and her two daughters, were camping in the office. But he promised to put me at the head of his waiting list and lent us a camp-bed and a screen and agreed to store my belongings. For the week which followed my guardian angel - as I always called him - slept in the tiny windowless dressing-room leading to the bathroom. A real furnace, hiding his nudity behind the screen. He refused to let me have the camp-bed and would not sleep in the main room because he snored and got up frequently during the night.

'The old bladder, you know. In your condition, my child, it is *most* important to have a good night's rest.'

I used to spend the day at Maurice's bedside. Major Hassett kept dwelling on the kidney and cardiac complications bound to follow *if* Maurice recovered. The July heat was affecting me. My legs were so swollen that there was no difference between my thighs and my ankles. I had to leave Delhi for a cooler place. Because of its altitude, Simla was out. This left Poona, where Maurice had friends. The Civil Surgeon had been with him in Sholapur, and Hari Singh, with whom Maurice had shared life for a whole year in Dhulia, was now posted in Poona. Johnny Bowman would look after me in Bombay while in transit.

Had my guardian angel not been in Civil Aviation I could not have arranged for Johnny to meet me in Bombay. India was in the grip of a postal strike. A pilot informed Johnny of my arrival and asked him to fix Poona for me.

Maurice was delirious when I took leave on my way to the station. Major Hassett's parting words still ring in my ears:

'Mrs Zinkin, you don't look well. You are so swollen because your foetus is dead.'

Johnny drove me straight to St George's Hospital where he had reserved a room for me in the private wing. Handing me detective stories he said he would let me know as soon as he had made arrangements with Hari Singh. On his morning round the doctor said hospital was no place for me. I was pregnant, not ill. He discharged me. It must have been lunch-time when I reached Johnny who sent me back to hospital. That evening the man in the next room died after a noisy agony. I heard everything: his death rattle, the sobbing widow . . . I dreamt it was Maurice who had died. In the morning I rang Premy, she was to be our baby's godmother. It did not take long before her mother arrived. Lady Rama Rau said that as Premy was expecting and I might be a diphtheria carrier, they had decided I should stay with her.

Not before I was installed in one of the luxurious bedrooms of the Port Trust House did I break down.

'My dear, in your condition, you must think of the baby. Everything will be all right, please don't cry.' The more Lady Rama Rau tried to cheer me up the more I wept.

The Rama Raus were wonderful. I might have been their daughter. Lady Rama Rau urged me to stay in Bombay and have the baby in the same clinic as Premy:

'Doctor Shirodkar is famous. Asha, my grand-daughter, was born there. You could not be looked after better anywhere. Doctor Shirodkar is not a Civil Surgeon, but it is well worth the money to get the best man.' But Maurice used to swear by the Poona Civil Surgeon. As soon as Johnny had arranged it I left for Poona.

Hari Singh met me at the station. His imposing bull-like shape and friendly smile filled me with confidence. Competence, reliability were writ large over his strong features.

'I have fixed you up with Mrs Haig. My wife is also expecting and she has gone to Bangalore to be with her mother. We live in Yeravda, some distance from town and I am out all day. I thought you would feel more comfortable with your own people. Mrs Haig lives in the Cantonment and she will look after you well.'

A major's widow, Mrs Haig turned out to be trumps. Descended from the famous Jacob of Jacobabad fame, she supplemented her widow's pension by taking lodgers.

Maurice had friends in Poona. In addition to those locally posted, like Hari Singh who was Conservator of Forests or Jack Clarence-Smith whose wife Mijeanne was French, there were those, like Bobby Dalal whom I already knew, who were up from Bombay for the summer recess.

The Civil Surgeon seemed competent. The baby appeared healthy. Walking helped my legs, provided I put my feet up whenever possible. I had another six weeks to go. Poona was heavenly cool. I began to knit for the baby. Had I been in Delhi, only nappies and vests would have been required. In Poona, woollens were essential.

Mijeanne, too, was expecting. I walked to her flat every day, stayed for lunch and walked back after tea. Bobby, who had a car, often dropped in to see me before dinner and took me for a spin. Hari Singh, a great one for betting on horses, took me to the races. Had I had news of Maurice all would have been well. Eventually a traveller brought a letter. Maurice was going to be discharged with six weeks' convalescence leave. Soon we would be together.

Mahatma Gandhi was staying in a Poona ashram. I had arranged to meet him after his prayer meeting on the 8th of August. Bobby Dalal offered to take me. We stopped off at the railway station on the way just in case Maurice was arriving. It was already dark. I tripped getting out of the car and began to pee, or so I thought, until I realized I was bleeding profusely. A clear case of placenta praevia. I told Bobby to drive me to the hospital. Instead, he took me back to Mrs Haig who sent him for the doctor. He was not at home and by the time they arrived I was floating in a pleasant state of semi-consciousness.

'I cannot hear the foetal heart', the Civil Surgeon announced. 'The baby is dead. The choice is between abortion and caesarian.' I knew he was right. I was bleeding to death. I chose caesarian. They did not show me the baby until I made a fuss. He looked like a blue baby.

The explanation for John's looks was given to us, after independence, when we stopped in Poona on our way to England.

'Now I can tell you. They thought the baby was dead. They were worried about you. When the sweeper woman came to clean the operating theatre she found John and spanked him until he screamed.' Mijeanne tried to help me find our benefactress. Locating a nameless woman in a big hospital, more than a year later, was like looking for a needle in a haystack.

Maurice arrived the day after John was born. My baby, no longer purple, was a fine big 8 months-old boy.

On the morning of the third day I woke up feeling bloated and parched but could not retain water. The Civil Surgeon prescribed morphine to dull the pain. A few hours later I had a second injection and was put on a glucose drip. The pain was unbearable. By the fifth day I began to scream louder than the women in the labour-room next door and kept the nurse so busy that Maurice had to give our son the bottle. The gap between injections shrank. The dosage increased. Despite the drip I was dying of a thirst made intolerable by the drumming of the monsoon and the dripping of a tap facing my bed. By the 9th day I had become a morphine addict, my mind leaving my body to float about. It was rather pleasant, especially since it was my body, not my mind, which screamed. I watched the room, the soiled sheets nurses no longer bothered to change . . . my hair caked in vomit . . . Maurice holding my hand, the *Poona*

Gazetteer open, unread on his lap. The baby in his cot.

It was the pathetic sight of my husband which saved me. I, who was screaming when injections were late, refused the next one. Without morphine I applied my mind.

I had a fairly rare complication: a paralysis of the gut. It was going to kill me. I should have died already. Soon my bowels would burst. The only hope to ease the pressure was to absorb as much of the gasses as possible, to restore the peristalsis. I sent Maurice to the chemist for activated charcoal and managed to keep it down.

The Civil Surgeon had warned Maurice's friends I would not last the night. Having given me up from the start he had been pumping morphine into me. He confessed it was a miracle that I survived.

My mind had left my body at the critical moment. An old friend, Monsieur Morel-Revoil, who had spent years in the East, once told me how he had survived himself.

'My guru taught me to free myself from my body by willpower. Without the mind, the body cannot die; but the body can kill the mind when it is inside the body. When I had that heart attack, I sent my mind - religious people would call it my soul - out and watched the heart attack. When it was over I reintegrated my body.'

The Sassoon Hospital in Poona was old-fashioned, dirty, badly run. Pie dogs wandered in and out of rooms. A baby in the night-nursery had half its face eaten by a bandicoot. Maurice hired an ayah to keep watch over John at night. The nursing was awful. I had bedsores. When my drip fell out the night nurse stuck it back into my left breast.

Born a month early, John only had the pink and blue shawl I had finished knitting. Molly Simms, the Collector's wife, organised hand-me-downs. With the help of Service wives, by the time we left the hospital, John was fully kitted out.

I can still recall the feeling of wonder as I watched the sun in the flowering trees lining the drive when the ambulance took us back to Mrs Haig. I was alive! We had a lovely baby! All was well!

Back in Delhi I began to pass clots. I had two curettings. We went to Indore to consult the Maharajah's gynaecologist who found nothing wrong.

'Better wait for your next home leave. Healing in India is more dodgey and, with luck, the bleeding may stop. But don't get pregnant,' were his parting words.

In London, where I stopped on my way to America to see my parents, I consulted Sir Cecil Wakeley. Without examining me, the Queen's gynaecologist diagnosed cancer of the womb and offered to remove it for a handsome fee. My father was practising medicine in New York. I decided to wait for his verdict. He curetted me and removed a long thread which was acting as a drain.

'If there are more, and they won't show on X-ray, you will have to have a hysterectomy.'

I had the operation in London. The operation cost nothing. It was performed on the first day of National Health. There were seven faulty stitches in my womb. Miss Basden, the surgeon, had made a second cut, parallel to the first, creating a furrow one inch wide and half a yard long, adding physical to emotional mutilation. I was barren, and disfigured, at thirty. Three months later, during the statutory check-up I complained of painful breasts.

'They will have to come off because of cancerous degeneration. In any case, breasts are a nuisance, they get in the way. That's why the Amazons invented mastectomy, to string their bows without hindrance. The only use for breasts is milk. Now that you can't have children it's no loss.' She booked me in at the hospital for the following Monday.

'What's the matter? You look like a ghost!' Maurice's mother asked.

'My breasts have to be removed on Monday.' It was Friday evening.

'Nonsense. We will get a second opinion!' she said.

15

My friend Indira

When I accompanied Maurice to Bombay I had insisted on going second class. We were broke. Inflation had cut his pay by a three quarters which the seventeen and a half percent marriage allowance did practically nothing to restore. ICS officers travelled first class and were entitled to one and a half times the railway fare to cover travelling expenses. I had a first class return ticket for the 36 miles between Kalyan and Bombay so that we would arrive together to be met by his Bombay staff. The only difference between first and second class was that we were six instead of four. The journey had been comfortable. Naturally, therefore, when Indira Gandhi invited me to spend a week with her in Mussoorie I went second class.

The journey was a nightmare. Summer heat had turned the carriage into an oven made infernal by the refusal of my five companions to open even one window and by the presence of three braziers filled with live coals. The clutter, not to mention half a dozen noisy and hyperactive infants, was indescribable. Bags of rice; countless boxes; half a dozen tin trunks; bedding rolls; cooking pots galore; four Ali Baba-sized earthen jars oozing water; jars of chutney; baskets of vegetables and two stone slabs to grind spices on. Two women squatted on the floor and began to fan the braziers blowing ashes over everything. The compartment had become a kitchen.

Cooking in a moving train is messy, especially with small children about. My clothes were splashed with oily, pungent, reddish-green gravy and the marks of small hands. It was past midnight by the time the food was ready. In such a confined space the smell was overpowering.

My companions did offer me to partake of their feast. But all I wanted was to sleep, if possible. Never again would I travel in a ladies' compartment. Never, on the many occasions in the years that followed when, as a foreign correspondent, I travelled second and even third class, did I have such appalling fellow travellers.

I owed my friendship with Indira to her aunt. Maurice was an old friend of Mrs Pandit's. When he went to Allahabad on duty she invited him to stay. While he was there she was summoned to Delhi and Maurice had asked her to bring something back for him; I have forgotton what. I packed whatever it was and walked across to the residence of Jawaharlal Nehru, with whom she was staying.

There was nobody at the gate or at the door, so I walked on and found myself in the drawing room. In a corner a young woman was reading a book which, I saw from the cover, was French. She was small, frail, wrapped in a sari. I made a noise and she looked up, startled. I was struck by her vulnerability. Thin face. Large eyes. Patrician nose marred by a small wart on the tip*. Self-effacing. Almost apologetic smile. Her voice was thin, high pitched, with a soft lilt.

I explained my presence and we began to chat about the book while a servant was sent to inform Mrs Pandit. Indira offered me a glass of sweet lime juice and we discovered that we had more than French in common. Her son Rajiv was not much older than mine, there was only a year between us and we shared the conviction that India should be free. By

*The wart was removed during her first visit to America.

the time Mrs Pandit let it be known that I could leave my parcel we had spent the best part of two hours together. 'Do come again any time', Indira said, walking me to the gate. I only had to cross the road, our hostel facing the Nehru residence. It did not take long before I became a fixture in that household; sometimes staying for lunch, often for tea.

Nehru looked so young . . . like Tyrone Power . . . in his presence I was tongue-tied. We never had a proper conversation. He got so used to seeing me that he would automatically stop his driver to give me a lift whenever he saw me walking alone. The perfect gentleman he could, at times, be catty. Very tall for an Indian woman, Mridula Sarabhai, a middle-aged spinsterly member of the Ahmedabad textile empire, was head over heels in love with him. She used to hang about adoringly, drinking his words, following him from room to room like a puppy. Pathetic rather than ridiculous in heavy Pathan sandals which enlarged her big feet. Mannish in a Punjabi outfit with loose trousers of coarse cotton, hair cut short, swarthy complexion, strong features, flat chest, deep voice. Unsexed.

'Can't somebody tell her to try to look like a woman?' Nehru, exasperated by that dog-like devotion, once asked Indira. But such outbursts were rare.

One of Nehru's faults was his inability to say 'No'. Indira and I were sipping sweet lime juice on the rocks one afternoon when an agitated servant asked her to come to the front gate. I followed her. A young man was standing in the drive, surrounded by a bedding-roll, tin trunks and a considerable supply of tinned US army disposal food in cardboard boxes.

'My name is M O Mathai. I ask nothing, no money, just a corner for myself and the privilege of serving Panditji. It is my mission in life to serve Panditji'. Refusing to leave he persuaded Indira to let him wait for her father's return. For a while M O Mathai camped in the Nehru compound, eating his own tins, a figure of fun. Gradually he wormed himself into the Prime Minister's good books, became his Personal Private Secretary and, within less than a decade, an Eminence Grise feared by many in high places.*

When it was too hot we would repair to Indira's bed-room, the only ground-floor bed-room in the house and, delight of delights, air-conditioned. Bliss! Air-conditioning, still exceptional, was a necessity for Indira. She had inherited her mother's constitution; pleurisy had sent her to a Davos sanatorium. She still had to rest every day and be careful not to overdo things.

'Father hates illness. He has such a robust constitution. He cannot be bothered with people who are ill.' A natural reaction from one whose wife had slowly died of consumption.

Indira was lonely. Her husband was in Lucknow, working for the *National Herald*, the family newspaper. Her father was very busy and most of the politicians who thronged to the house were old. There was a generation gap in the Congress, probably one of the reasons why Indira had so few friends. She was not only lonely, she was also diffident. Her childhood and adolescence had been unhappy: overcast by her mother's ill-health; disrupted by the political activities which kept sending her father to jail - even her mother had been imprisoned once. Deprived of children with whom to play - why was not clear - she used to harangue her dolls, recounting for their benefit the horrors of British tyranny. Never long enough in one school, one place, or one college, to make the life-long friends who can act a crutches in times of need, she had come to lean more and more on Feroz Gandhi. A young Parsee from her home-town, of her own age, as a child he had been part of the Bandar Sena, the Monkey Brigade, Indira's band of children messengers.

Indira, who adored her mother, still resented the way her aunts had patronised Kamala, 'treating her like a nobody because she was not fluent in English.' She resented, too,

* Eventually there was a scandal and he was sacked.

the way her father had neglected his wife. This resentment explained why, in her bed-room there was a photograph of Kamala which she treated like an ikon, and none of her father.

'Feroz was devoted to Mother. Unlike Father he realized, while she was alive, what an exceptional person she was.' When she found Feroz in England after her mother's death, she fell in love. She used to talk with pride of his achievements. There had been that photograph he sold to *The Daily Telegraph*, or was it the *Daily Mail* ? Of her marriage she did not speak. I got the impression it was not happy. Feroz and Nehru did not get on. A certain coarseness in his son-in-law grated upon Nehru's aristocractic temperament. Tension existed between the two men, a tension even I could feel on the odd occasions when Feroz came to Delhi.

When Nehru called her, Indira left Feroz to become her father's hostess. This involved much housekeeping. As a hostess she remained in the background, allowing others to shine, standing literally back behind people, as if to hide. She was diffident, patently starved of affection. Except for a few old servants, like everyone else, Nehru took her for granted. Indira was not only diffident. She was also embittered.

One day I found her in tears. In anticipation of Independence Delhi had become a busy diplomatic centre, hostessing a full time job. Mrs Pandit had come to relieve her niece who was in the last stages of pregnancy. Leaving the domestic chores to Indira, on the ground that the servants were not hers and that she did not know her way about the kitchens, Mrs Pandit had taken the downstairs bed-room, the only air-conditioned one. Indira had to drag herself up a long flight of stairs and stay in a hot room a few days before Sanjay was born.

Instead of protesting, Indira was weeping.

A few years later, in Lucknow, during an international conference inaugurated by Nehru I had another example of the way she used to be overlooked. There was a big reception in the gardens of the University. Not having seen Indira for some time I was shocked. She looked so ill that I expected her to faint any minute. She whispered that Rajiv and Sanjay, the children, were both ill and that she had spent the last couple of nights at their bedsides but that her father still expected her to hostess.

'Your place is in bed. I will tell him.' By then I was no longer tongue-tied in Nehru's presence. He sent her to bed and asked me to hostess instead. The trouble was thoughtlessness, not lack of affection. The Prime Minister of India, at the time of that conference, was engaged, as he explained at length, after the guests had gone, presumably for the the benefit of my British readers, in a fight against the old guard for the leadership of the Congress Party. Of his affection for his only child I had no doubt. Indeed, on the occasion in Amritsar, when Indira's car got stranded during a mammoth procession of vociferously friendly demonstrators, Nehru flared up with anxious rage calling the head of the CID 'gadda', donkey, in public - a grave insult - before rushing himself to her rescue.

The day I found Indira in a plain white sari I teased her.

'Why are you dressed like an ayah?' Ayahs usually wore plain cotton saris with a border. Indira's sari had no border and I should have asked her why she was dressed like a widow, since Hindu widows wear plain white saris without borders; but comparing her to a widow would have been in bad taste.

'This is not an ayah's sari. It is Bapu's (Gandhi's) wedding present. One of my most precious possessions. He spun the yarn himself.' The sari was fairly fine, with irregularities in the weave due to breaks in the thread. Indira added 'You know, Taya, Bapu is such a wonderful person. I would go to him for advice if I was in trouble. He is so full of love. Nobody is too small, no problem too trifling for him.'

'Did he approve when you got married?' I could not help

asking. Maurice had told me how bitterly Mrs Pandit had resented her niece marrying 'the son of the family grocer.' The Gandhis owned the largest general store in Allahabad.

'Father did not consult Bapu. He knew he would object because Feroz is not a Hindu. Father did not want what happened to my aunt to happen to me. I am sure that if Father had been at home instead of abroad at the time when she eloped things would have been different. That is why, in my case, he presented Bapu with a fait accompli.' Indira then told me what had happened before Mrs Pandit got married.

I already knew Mrs Pandit's sad story from Mrs Naidu who had insisted that Sayed Hussein, not Jinnah, was the father of Pakistan. Sardar Panikkar, too, had told me the story. His explanation for Motilal's attitude, so out of character for a near agnostic many of whose best friends were Muslims, was that Sayed Hussein was his own illegitimate son. But I have no idea whether this is true.

Indira met me at the terminus. One had to climb the last bit to the house on foot or by rickshaw. Within Mussoorie cars were prohibited.

'My goodness! What a sight! What happened ?'

Washing in the train had been out of the question. The bathroom attached to our compartment had been turned into a cluttered kitchen dump. Indira was indignant.

'Tomorrow we will go to the Charleville. I know the manager. I am sure he can arrange for someone to give you a lift back to Delhi by car. And if it means staying a bit longer, all the better. Leave it to me.'

Indira was staying in the guest-house of Sir Padampat Singhania, a mansion even more luxurious than that of Sir Bagchand Soni in Ajmer. There was a private safe in each suite. I had a delicious bath and a rest before lunch. As in Delhi the food was mostly Western and rather bland. Nothing exotic. After a siesta we wandered off to the bazaar.

The perfect hostess, Indira had fallen in with my wish to get Indian vegetables. During my year in the West Indies I had become partial to ladies' fingers - okra in the US, kalaloo bango in Creole and bhindi in Hindi. We got some, as well as drumsticks and lotus stems. Indira said she would ask the children's ayah to cook them. Indira had no experience of cooking and left it to cooks. The one she had brought with her specialised in Western food.

'Cooking is so complicated. In Delhi we have a Muslim as well as a Hindu cook. And then, there are all the taboos. Would you believe it, we have a great-aunt who brings her own cooking pots and pans when she comes to stay and insists on cooking her food on the verandah. She will not set foot in the kitchens, which she considers to be dens of iniquity, cesspits of pollution. We eat meat and eggs! She is so orthodox that nobody is allowed to watch her eating.'

In the evening we listened to gramophone records and looked at an album of photographs, mostly of herself with her mother during their stay abroad. Indira was so thin that her nose looked disproportionately long between hollowed cheeks and sunken eyes. One of her pictures, in pyjamas, with the hip-bones showing, reminded me of Belsen.

'That was at Oxford.' Mistaking the expression on my face, Indira went on to reminisce. She had been invited to address Indian students. 'I heard someone shout: "She doesn't speak, she squeaks!" I felt terrible.'

When I watched her first public speech at the Amritsar Session of the All India Congress Committee a few years later I was reminded of her Oxford squeak. She was still self-effacing and shrill but she no longer squeaked. By the mid-fifities, when she became Congress President, she had at last conquered the shyness of her gawky youth to become a woman in full bloom.

On our way to the Charleville Hotel Indira was accosted by a weird apparition.

'Indu, Indu, How terrible! *how awful!* What a tragedy for India and the world!' Bird-faced, bat-like in a sombre kaftan, tears streaming down wrinkled cheeks, she was clinging to my friend. Between her sobs we managed to drag out the cause of that dramatic sorrow: it was the death of Rabindranath Tagore.

'But,' Indira exclaimed, 'he died over a year ago.' The bat had just heard the news. Consoled, she wiped her face with the folds of her kaftan and made us promise not to leave the Charleville without dropping in for a cup of tea.

After the Hotel manager said he would fix me with a lift we went to the basement where Mrs Brunner, a painter refugee from Hitler, was camping in a minute room with her daughter and a pet hen. The hen's feathers and droppings had turned that room into a pig-sty. Declining tea, Indira insisted on being shown the latest pictures. Elizabeth, whom her mother treated like a child although she was already middle-aged, was by far the better painter. She also had a sense of humour. She submitted a life-size poster of an igloo to the Delhi Low-Cost Housing Exhibition. Before leaving the Brunners, Indira bought a calf's head by Elizabeth.

'I shall send someone to collect it.' As the Brunners were obviously hard up she sent them a bag of rice, a basket of fruit and Indian sweets.

A couple of days later the Hotel manager sent word that I should be at the car park, beside car number such and such at 2 pm on the day I was planning to leave. Mr Smith, a senior US diplomat would drive me back to Delhi.

It was a leisurely week. Walks, playing with Rajiv, winding the gramophone, listening to music, trips to the bazaar where I bought a small bamboo arm-chair for our son and, since Indira liked it, one for Rajiv. Beside reading, chatting and, in my case, knitting, we did nothing but laze. On the last evening we decided to beat it up.

Indira lent me one of her more glamorous saris. I put a

red mark on my forehead, did my hair in a bun enlarged by a jasmin garland and borrowed some of the ayah's silver ornaments. Being sun-tanned, I looked as Indian as Indira. We set off for the Blue Danube, a night-club which featured a telephone on each table. The table's number lit up so that callers could be identified. Half way through the evening a tall man with a crew cut came in with a woman.

'What do you bet it's Mr Smith?'

'Let's find out.' Taking me up on it Indira dialled the number of the couple's table. After spotting where the call was coming from the man did not lift the receiver. We tried again without success. I scribbled on a piece of paper 'Are you Mr Smith?' and asked a waiter to deliver my message. Crumpling the note, the man turned a virtuous back in our direction. Forgetting that the name Smith is so often used in a particular way, it had not crossed our minds that we were being mistaken for tarts.

The next day we were waiting by the car when Mr Smith, the self-same, arrived with his wife.

16

Pogroms and paraphernalia

The war was over. India was straining towards independence. Asia was in ferment. It was an exciting time and we were part of it. There were the anti-British agitation, the Cabinet Mission, Jinnah's Direct Action Day, the Asian Conference, the Referendum in the NWFP, the Handing Over of Power . . . and the Partition riots.

I used to cycle to Old Delhi to ferret for curios in the Thieves' Market at the foot of the magnificent Moghul mosque, the Jamna Masjid. There, heaped in the open, was everything from rusty nails and lavatory bowls to genuine jewelry, often stolen. Half the fun was the haggle and the hope of finding a treasure, I never did. From the Thieves' Market I would cycle to the Silver Market for the sheer pleasure of watching the silversmiths at work in their cubicles. Then, on to the Vegetable Market where fruit and vegetables artistically displayed in colourful pyramids tempted custom. The day I lost my way in a maze of narrow alleys I had my first taste of the anti-British agitation which was sweeping India.

To avoid colliding with a cow I jumped off my bike flattening myself against the wall. The handle-bar touched the sacred beast's bloated paunch. Appearing from nowhere, a handful of urchins shouting abuse began to pelt me with garbage. In my haste to flee I grazed my knee and fell into the gutter to the delight of these budding nationalists. I did not venture into Old Delhi so long as the agitation lasted.

My next experience was in Sind. Maurice and I had stopped to change trains in Hyderabad City. There was a long wait. Fascinated by the sight of the ventilation chimneys which are so typical of that old town, I suggested we go sight-seeing. The Army Chaplain who was sharing our compartment came too. These chimney tops were extraordinary, shaped like slim angular funnels, most picturesque. Wandering in the old city we entered an open space and ran into a small and noisy procession. Two strapping youths were dragging a donkey. The donkey's nostrils, torn by a rope, were bleeding profusely. A garland of shoes and a billboard dangled from its neck. A lout kept kicking the poor beast, viciously twisting its tail, and prodding its genitals while half a dozen hooligans kept hitting it with sticks.

'This must stop at once', I exclaimed. The Chaplain warned.

'It says "Angresi" (English) in Urdu on that board. This is a political demonstration. One has to be very careful not to pour oil on the fire. Besides, they are more than twenty, better walk on.'

'But that poor donkey! I don't care about the politics. It's the donkey I mind about.' Like all French girls reared on Madame de Sévigné's Mémoires d'un Ane I nurse a very soft spot for donkeys. Before Maurice could stop me I pushed the miscreants back, carefully removed the rope from the torn nostrils and with my headscarf improvised a dressing. This done I gave those swine a piece of my mind in kitchen Urdu. They listened in pin-drop silence and walked away abashed, leaving the donkey. I had been lucky. Not so everybody.

Doctor Ronald, Sardar Patel's* physician, scared by the agitation, had decided to return to Europe. He was dissuaded by the Sardar.

*Sardar Patel the chief organiser of the Congress Party became India's first Deputy Prime Minister.

'He said I had nozeeng to fear - "You are German" he said, "zees is an anti-Breetish demonstratzion" and zo I vas quite safe. Like a fool I believed him!' Doctor Ronald was attacked, his car smashed, his nose broken, his cheek slashed.

Six months after my arrival Sir Stafford Cripps led a Cabinet Mission to Delhi with the awoved purpose of finding ways to hand over power to a united India. Maurice, despite his relative lack of seniority, became involved with the Mission. I was still too new to the intricacies of Indian politics to understand what was happening. That is why my recollections are hazy and patchy.

Guy Wint, a friend of Maurice's, had told Woodrow Wyatt to contact us. Woodrow, the junior-most member of the Mission and its dog's body, was quick to make our quarters his second home, dropping in unexpectedly at the Club, usually at meal-times. On his advice, Sir Stafford spent a whole morning picking Maurice's brains.

Woodrow was the only divorced person of my own age I then knew. I found him fascinating. A brilliant conversationalist, he thrived on a mixture of boyish charm and impudence made tolerable because his was an original, if at times poaching, mind; a mind still devoid of its later pomposity.

'Taya, there's a hole in my sock.' Taking off his shoe, he tossed me the sock, mimicking a dog begging for sugar, 'darn it please.' While I did so he told me what happened in Bombay. 'I booped dreadfully. After seeing Jinnah, I called on Gandhi and called him 'Mister Jinnah.' The old boy took it frightfully well I must say. 'Young man, you flatter me' he giggled and throughout our talk gave me the feeling that he minded about me as a person. Quite a contrast from Jinnah, who is frightfully aloof.'

One evening Woodrow brought Arthur Bottomley, the Under-Secretary of State, to dinner. I cannot remember what the men talked about, only that Mr Bottomley made a strong impression of unimaginatively earnest dependability. By contrast, Lord Pethwick-Lawrence, whom I met at parties, struck me as a small flotsam out of his depth. No wonder they called the Secretary of State for India 'Pathetic-Lawrence' behind his back. I still blush in retrospect at my ignorance when Mr A V Alexander, the Mission's Defence member, asked - perhaps in a desperate attempt at conversation - what I thought would happen to the Gurkhas after independence and dropped his sandwich on the lawn when I replied: 'What are Gurkhas?'

As far as I was concerned, most of the excitement during the Mission's stay was vicarious. Maurice was excited, but not half as much as Kitty Shiva Rao or Fori Nehru. We had moved to Simla, thanks to the concern Maurice's boss had shown for my health, and everybody was there.

Bob Stimson of the BBC, a contemporary of Maurice's at Cambridge, was staying at the Cecil Hotel, which had become the nexus of the political world. Frequently his guests, we hob-nobbed with the mighty in the dining-room. Sardar Panikkar was up for the Chamber of Princes. Without fully understanding what was going on I could see that history was in the melting-pot. Kitty and Fori, with whom I often spent an afternoon, were redolent with rumours which usually emanated from 'Asaf'. Asaf Ali, whom I never met, was, according to Maurice, paid by the Home Department to report on meetings of the Congress Party's Working Committee. This, Maurice said, was beneficial to the Congress because what was said in private was far more reasonable than the public pronouncements.

It was a confusing time all round. Leaders going back and forth on their word. Leaked telegrams. Explosive press conferences. No sooner had Nehru accepted something than Jinnah backed out and when Jinnah agreed it was Gandhi's turn to say *No*. Enough to drive the Viceroy and all concerned to distraction. I remember Panikkar saying, half in jest, that Cripps' approach was all wrong:

'Sir Stafford and Gandhiji have so many cranks in common,

from austerity to vegeterianism, from teetotalling to religious earnestness. They are made for each other. What Sir Stafford should do is get Jinnah to agree first and then force Gandhiji's hand by announcing that he will fast unto death.'

When Jinnah launched his Direct Action Day we were in Poona. The full horror of the mass killings which took place in Calcutta did not hit us until we got back to Delhi. My friend Stella had fled after finding the head of her peon* on her desk.

'Poor Gangaram's face was crawling with flies and cockroaches! My papers were soaked in blood, a whole month's work destroyed! There was blood everywhere. Taya, you won't believe it, the streets were full of bodies. And the police were doing nothing, absolutely nothing, just looking the other way. It was unbelievable! Unbelievable!' Estimates of the dead ranged from four thousand five hundred to thirty thousand. The Muslim Chief Minister of Bengal had planned the massacre. By the third day, Calcutta's taxi drivers, most of whom were Sikhs, had organised themselves and, with the help of Hindus, went on the rampage, killing Muslims in retaliation. It was an inexcusably long week before the British Governor, an ex-trade-union official, called in the Army.

The Calcutta killings triggered off a pendulum of retaliation which kept swinging, with escalating horror, to culminate, almost to the day, a year later, in the Partition riots.

In the end, more Muslims than Hindus and Sikhs had been killed in Calcutta. So Hindus were attacked in Noakhali, a remote district of East Bengal.

Noakhali stands out in the saga of communal atrocities because, for the first time in such riots, women were raped. Even during the Mutiny not a single British woman was

*messenger boy.

raped; killed yes, raped never. Hence indeed, the fuss in 'Passage to India' when Miss Quested imagined that an Indian had made a pass at her. The news of the Noakhali rapes spread across India like wild-fire.

'They raped mothers in front of their children, then made them eat beef and converted them to Islam. What is to become of the poor things now?' Kitty's husband had returned from Noakhali where Mridula Sarabhai was opening a rehabilitation centre for these raped women. Kitty was beside herself. 'You see, Taya, even if the husband is alive he will have nothing to do with her. She is polluted for life, not just defiled, polluted. No Hindu rite can purify her. Outcast, abandoned, an object of revulsion, an innocent victim. I admire Mridula for her initiative but I cannot see how these poor women can ever go back to their families.' Probably less than three hundred had been raped but half a dozen would have been enough, so enormous was the outrage. Women are held in great respect in India.

To avenge Noakhali, Muslims were butchered in Bihar. Maurice used to say that communal rioting only stops when casualties are equal on both sides.

Mahatma Gandhi came out of his self-imposed semi-retirement. Leaving the Sweeper's Colony, his Delhi residence, he went to Bengal. His Inner Voice told him not to fast unto death. Nobody was in the mood to listen. He announced he would go on a half-fast, eating six hundred calories a day, until the killing stopped. On that daily ration, two hundred calories short of the vital minimum for those in bed, he set out for the villages of East Bengal, by train, by boat, on foot, preaching brotherly love. Village after village had been devastated, houses burnt. Children roamed, orphaned, terrified. Gandhi eventually settled in a Muslim village and announced he would die there. After a whole month on half-fast the killings stopped. Hindu-Muslim unity was restored.

'I have been rescued from the jaws of death', he wrote to

Mira Bhen, his adopted daughter. When sectarian killings flared up again, Gandhi continued to walk the villages, this time without success.

'Mine will prove a voice in the wilderness but I cannot remain silent. I have no desire to prolong my life. I wish to die in harness, taking the name of God with my last breath,' he wrote in prophetic despair. In the rest of India communal tension rose as rioting spread, first to the NWFP and then to the Punjab, but Bengal remained quiet. Gandhi's pilgrimage had not been in vain. In Delhi, extraordinary as it seems in retrospect, life went on as usual.

For me the highlight of early Spring 1947 was the Asian Relations Conference. Called by Pandit Nehru it brought together leaders from Asia and the Middle East. It was a big event, the first of its kind. A warning to the West and the Iron Curtain that the Third World was coming into being and could no longer be taken for granted. Mrs Naidu, the Chairman of the Conference had asked me to help, as interpreter. It was a busy fortnight, filled to the brim. So much happened in so short a time that what stands vividly out in my memory are the incongruities.

There was the European monk swathed in a Buddhist robe asking me at a Viceregal reception if I, too, was gatecrashing. Holding a plate filled to perilous heights with cakes and sandwiches he added, with a thick Teutonic accent 'one must poutsch, poutsch, always in zees life' and he grabbed more food to stuff in his shoulder-bag.

There was the Cultural Programme at Pandit Nehru's residence. A makeshift stage in the garden with sofas, armchairs, chairs and mats in a semi-circle. Everything was dark, except the stage. Mountbatten, who had landed that very day, sat in a comfortable armchair in the middle of the front row. Begun at ten o' clock, the programme was, like Indian films, dragging on. Hindu dances, Muslim dances, tribal dances, folk dances, vocal and instrumental music . . .

Having translated French into English and vice-versa for the best part of the day I was tired. When the Kathak dancer regaled us with an encore followed by a second dose of Bharatnatyam and a repeat of the Manipuri ballet I asked my neighbour when it would end. He said that it should have ended long ago. But the Viceroy was enjoying himself and nobody could leave before he did. I crept to the front row. Mountbatten was fast asleep. I tripped against his legs. He looked at his watch and exclaimed: 'Good God! It's three o'clock!' and left.

The closing session of the Conference was a grand affair in a huge marquee. VIPs, delegates, interpreters sat on a rostrum raised some six feet above the invitees, estimated to run into thousands. There were many gate-crashers and not enough seats. Altercations and scuffles ensued. Mrs Naidu's appeals on the loud speaker were drowned in the din. Nehru jumped from the rostrum, dived into the central alley and, grabbing a head in each hand, banged them together. Ploughing his way forward, he banged more heads until order was restored. It was an extraordinary spectacle.

'Comme il est jeune et vigoureux!' whispered the Persian delegate. We had been fellow students at the Sorbonne before the war. There were no Persian interpreters and he had given me the gist of his speech beforehand.

'I don't think much of your Persian,' Mrs Naidu teased me, 'Your translation was not very good.' I told Padmaja how impressed I was by her mother's command of Persian. She burst out laughing:

'Typical of Mother. She was pulling your leg. She doesn't know Persian.'

Gandhi, who had come from Noakhali, was very frail and weak. His voice was faint, barely audible. What he said was unintelligible, at least as far as I, sitting a couple of feet away, was concerned. I was not able to translate his speech to the Francophone delegates. Except for 'atom bomb' which kept recurring, what he said was blurred by the loudspeaker's exaggeration of the sibilant sizzles of his toothlessness.

Mrs Naidu delivered the closing address. She was magnificent. Dramatically draped in a splendid sari. Charismatic. She spoke in the ringing tones of the accomplished orator. I can still hear her 'plucking stars from the sky.' The audience was deeply moved. So was I. The notes I took contained nothing but lyricism.

Half-way through the Conference, the delegate from Cambodia attached herself to me. Petite, shrivelled but neat, she remained silent, in sharp contrast to the delegate from Annam (now Vietnam) who spoke torrentially. Exasperated by his outflow she whispered:

'Victor Hugo and Proust rolled into one to produce what? Hot air! Remember Boileau's "ce qui se conçoit bien s'énonce clairement." What a sad reflection on his education.'

I invited her to tea. The head-mistress of a girl's school, or an inspectress, she was either a spinster or a widow. All I remember is that she was a Royal Princess and a staunch French nationalist. Talk of colonial exploitation angered her. Except for her face, she was out-and-out French. She loathed Annam and Siam, loved Napoléon, Henri Quatre, Jeanne D'Arc . . . According to her the Indians were ungrateful. They did not appreciate the benefits of colonisation's civilising mission.

'Without France, we would still be in the Middle-Ages.'

'But what about the great Temples of Angkor?' I had been tremendously impressed by the replica at the Colonial Exhibition of 1937.

'Precisely. The French are proud of what they are preserving. And they are showing it to the world. France brought us peace, prosperity and with the French language a window on the world and progress. If they go it will be a sad day for Indochina. Like dogs, they will be at each others' throats and, as always, it is the people, not the politicians, who will suffer. Back to the Middle-Ages we will go, but with one difference: better weapons. *Chère amie*, let us pray that the French never leave Indochina.'

Panikkar, who also called me *chère amie*, in memory of his Paris days, asked me to invite two delegates to dinner.

'We will dine downstairs of course, then I shall leave. They have something to discuss. Be an angel, take them upstairs to your apartments for coffee.'

Our 'apartments' consisted of one large room with a terrace and a short narrow corridor leading to a utility-sized bathroom. Not much space for the three of us. The baby's ayah and the bearer slept elsewhere. I had isolated the nursery with a screen and a wardrobe. The rest was our bedroom, our drawing-room and his play-room. Promotion came when we were due to get a C-class house, putting us at the bottom of the B-class house queue. A C-class house would have been the answer to our dreams. B-class houses were, if anything, too large for us. After all Indira Gandhi lived in a B-class house when she became Prime Minister. As it was, we were lucky to have one large room. Zeenat's hotel room was less than half the size of ours; she, too, had a baby and her husband was senior to Maurice.

The delegates Panikkar had invited were George Yé, China's Foreign Minister, and Sultan Shariar of Indonesia. The table d'hôte in Fonseca's hostel was excellent. Panikkar had brought champagne . . . Upstairs, as it was time for John's bottle, I left 'my' guests to their coffee. Pacing the room to make John burp I got snippets of their conversation. The Kuomintang was being asked to supply arms in preparation for Indonesia's fight for independence.

I owe my first taste of journalism to the Referendum in the North West Frontier Province.

The NWFP is special. It is inhabited by Pathans whose tribal organisation is similar, in many ways, to that of Scottish clans. Although Muslim, the Pathans were closer to the Indian National Congress than to Jinnah's Muslim League.

Their charismatic leader, Abdul Gafar Khan, known as 'the Frontier Gandhi', was a disciple of the Mahatma. In 1931 when Gandhi started a Civil Disobedience Movement, the Red Shirts, Abdul Gafar Khan's followers, mobilised en masse to march on the capital of the NWFP. Iskander Mirza*, had regaled us over dinner with a story of that massive demonstration. The tribes had been flocking towards Peshawar where, in defiance of a ban on processions, they planned to court arrest by the thousands. Iskander, who was the Deputy Commissioner at the time, realized he could not stem the flow with the small police force at his disposal. I can still hear him describe how he sent the encamped tribesmen huge cauldrons of spicy food, generously laced with castor oil.

'There was no demonstration, The Red Shirts were far too busy shitting!'

When Bob Stimson said he was going to Peshawar for the Referendum I told him Iskander's story.

'Why don't you come along as my assistant? They won't allow me near the women's polling booths, but they will let you. My listeners in England will be interested to hear how Pathan women voted for the first time in their lives.' We shared the coupé he had reserved on the Frontier Mail and were met next morning by Phil Talbot of the *Chicago Tribune*. Since the BBC and the *Tribune* did not compete, Bob and Phil pooled information and shared me.

The first thing we did was to interview the Khan brothers. Dr Khan Saheb, the younger brother, was a politician, unlike his elder brother who was a social reformer like Gandhi. A less similar pair would have been hard to find. Dr Khan Saheb, loquacious, short for a Pathan, podgy, neatly dressed like Pandit Nehru. The Frontier Gandhi, tall, bony, clad in coarse white handspun, head shaven, ascetic, taciturn. Both were equally critical of the Referendum

*later Governor General of Pakistan.

and had instructed the Red Shirts to boycott it.

'We should have been given a third option, not just a choice between accession to India or to Pakistan. What we want is Pakhtoonistan, an independent state. We are not Indians. We are Pathans. We have nothing in common with Punjabis, be they Muslim or Hindu. We are not going to vote.' They argued that the strength of the boycott would prove to the British that the Referendum was not valid. To show the size of their following they would march peacefully through the town once the voting was over.

While Phil and Bob wrote up their despatches, I wandered through the town. The old city was very romantic. Stalls elaborately stacked with fruit from temperate and tropical climes; water melons the size of side-cars, pyramids of ruby-red pomegranates . . . and everyhere tall men with biblical faces, hennaed beards, embroidered waistcoats, floating pantaloons, cartridge belts, rifles slung over shoulder . . . ready for parts in a Cecil B de Mille production of Gunga Din. Even pubescent boys wore guns. Iskander Mirza had not exaggerated. They did look fierce: 'They make their guns in backyard factories, very good ones too,' he had complained, saying it was impossible to control fire-arms on the Frontier. I visited a couple of small work-shops. Smithies, instead of shoeing horses, armed Pathans. After a while I strayed into a big carpet shop. A pair of rugs caught my admiration. So obviously expensive. So far above our means. I enthused freely.

'The Governor Saheb is a collector. He offered me four thousand five hundred rupees for the pair. Fool that I am, I would not go below seven thousand five hundred. And now there will be rioting, my shop will be looted or burnt and only Allah-willing shall I reach Kabul alive. If only I had taken the Governor Saheb's money!'

We called on the Governor the next day. Maurice had been a junior member of a small study group in Delhi to which he had belonged, so he asked us to stay for lunch. When I mentioned the rugs His Excellency confirmed the Afghan's story, they were 'exquisite'; unfortunately he could not afford the price.

I bought one of the rugs with a cheque on Delhi which was eventually cashed in Kabul. The shop was burnt. Could I have got the pair? In answer to a newspaper advertisement I had sold our shotgun for one thousand rupees, a price reflecting the tension in India as independence was approaching.

Buying that rug still dwarfs my recollection of the Referendum, but not that of our trip to Nandikotal - the British enclaved garrison on the way to the Afghan border. The Sikh taxi driver had warned. Only the road was in British India; the rest was un-administered tribal territory. The tribesmen, he said, were fierce in the defence of their freedom; so fierce that it was necessary, from time to time, to bomb villages from the air.

Picturesque, the villages stood in the distance, on either side of the road, mini-fortresses with crenellated turrets and battlements. The landscape, barren, stark and rugged, was dotted with mementoes to Beau Geste inscribed on plaques in the granite gorges which strangle the road as it winds its way to Afghanistan. Phil, who wanted to photograph a fortified village, asked the driver to stop. We got out. Unlike Bob who spent his penny beside the car, I made for a nearby boulder. Barely half-way a volley of shots fired from all sides propelled me back to the road. The driver said my dress had saved my life.

'Pathans first class shots, Memsahib, Pathans don't miss.'

The piece I wrote for Bob after spending the day in the ladies' enclosure watching women discard the tents inside which they hid from male view, must have been overwritten, stuffed with clichés like chrysalises becoming butterflies. It was nice of Bob to say he would use it and pay me twenty rupees.

Back in Delhi time was running out. Faster than expected.

Nehru, it has been said, did not think India would be independent before 1954. Faster than first announced Mountbatten brought the date of the transfer of power forward in the hope it might halt administrative disintegration and prevent civil war. By now Pakistan, once the dream of the poet Iqbal, was in the making.

Cut into two pieces, separated by a thousand miles of Indian territory, could such a State be viable? Muslims in the Congress, as well as Hindus, maintained that Pakistan, on its own, would collapse. It had no industries, no urban middle class. Jinnah's followers had not given the matter much thought. Even the British had doubts. It was widely believed that, without a Customs Union with India, Pakistan could not survive.

One morning, over breakfast, I asked Maurice if Pakistan could survive. Finance Communications in which he was the Deputy Financial Adviser was grinding to a standstill because Liaquat Ali, the Finance Minister and Jinnah's heir, was not going to sanction expenditure which might benefit India at Pakistan's future expense. To kill time and satisfy his own curiosity, Maurice spent the following fortnight perusing the All India Digest of Statistics. The statistics proved that Pakistan was not only viable but in a far stronger foreign exchange position than India. It was surplus in food. It grew most of the jute and some of the tea and much of the long-staple cotton of the sub-continent. He wrote a paper which he showed first of all to HM Patel, the Cabinet Secretary, under whom he had worked in Textile Control during the war. Patel, known as 'HM', did not ask Maurice to keep his discovery to himself. Maurice then showed his paper to Alan Campbell-Johnson, a Cambridge friend on Mountbatten's staff, and to Chowdhury Mahomed Ali, his senior in the Ministry of Finance, and a future Prime Minister of Pakistan. Finally, Maurice sent a copy of his paper, privately, to Geoffrey Crowther of *The Economist*.

During the final negotiations preceding Partition, when

Sardar Patel urged Liaquat Ali to enter into a Customs Union with India, Liaquat Ali refused, quoting Maurice's paper.

'The Viability of Pakistan' cost us £500, perhaps £5,000 in today's money.

At Independence the British Government gave members of the ICS £500 in compensation for loss of career for every year of service up to sixteen. Maurice had less than six weeks to complete his ninth year. He had volunteered to go on for a while but his services were smartly terminated on the 15th of August by Sardar Patel although he stayed on, without pay, till the worst of the Emergency in Delhi was over. By then he had more than made up the year. The Secretary of the ICS Association, none other than 'HM', pleaded with Sardar Patel to extend Maurice's tenure by six weeks to no avail. HMG, stingy as usual, benefitted.

Long before 'The Viability of Pakistan', we had decided we would like to stay in India. India was our home. Both India and the future Pakistan had indicated they would welcome certain people staying on, if only for a transition period. With only nine years service, Maurice had reached a critical stage in his career. At his suggestion I asked Indira to find out from her father whether we should stay. The answer had been negative. Had Maurice been in the Judiciary, or in one of the Provinces, things might have been different. In Delhi, particularly in the Finance and Commerce Pool, which had so many dealings with the outside world, the cream was bound to go to Indians.

If Maurice was not wanted in India, he was in hot demand in Pakistan. At one cocktail party Liaquat Ali spent the best part of an hour convincing me to bring pressure on Maurice to opt for Pakistan. Pakistan, he said, needed people like Maurice, it was terribly short of administrative talent. He could guarantee quick promotion and an interesting career.

'If Zinkin was here, I would tell him myself.' Maurice was in London for a reconstruction interview. 'Tell him not to jump at a job in the British Civil Service. I can offer him much better. Anything he wants. That paper on the viability of Pakistan was brilliant!' Liaquat Ali could be persuasive. To clinch his offer he added: 'I can personally guarantee that, as long as I live, your husband will have any job he wants.' I liked Liaquat Ali but could not help asking:

'How long will you live?' Getting up from the sofa on which we sat he bowed slightly:

'You are right. One must not build on imponderables. But do tell him, promise.' Was it premonition? Pakistan's first Prime Minister was assassinated in 1951.

From London Maurice cabled: 'OFFERED COLONIAL OFFICE STOP HOME EDITORSHIP ECONOMIST AND UNILEVER STOP ADVISE LOVE'. I cabled back 'ECONOMIST LOVE'. He chose Unilever.

17

Freedom's holocaust

On the 14th August, at midnight, I stood beside Maurice to watch the Viceroy hand over power to India. The Mountbattens were regal, Nehru Churchillian. I was moved to tears, proud of England, proud of India, sad to leave.

The next morning Himalayan disorder overtook the planned pageantry as euphoric crowds, estimated at over a million, streamed, lava-like, into the grounds. Nothing like it had ever been seen before. My friend Hélène, conscious of the etiquette required from the wife of a French Military Attaché had imported clothes from Paris for the occasion. She lost one shoe and her new hat. Her elegantly trimmed organdie dress was torn to shreds. Like most of us she never reached the VIP enclosure. Alan Campbell-Johnson later regaled us with Mountbatten's ordeal. The open gilded ceremonial carriage was swamped, carried on a human sea.

'You won't believe it, a baby peed on Her Excellency's lap!' Mountbatten himself is on record as having abandoned all ceremonial plans. Four Indian ladies with their children, the Polish wife of a British Officer and an Indian pressman climbed into his carriage to avoid being crushed while Nehru sat 'on the front hood, like a schoolboy.' Never had pandemonium been friendlier.

The atmosphere in Delhi during the preceding week had been almost festive. There had been a Viceregal reception in the Sunken Garden, the last Viceregal reception, and a series of farewell parties for friends and colleagues going to Pakistan. At the Imperial Delhi Gymkhana Club, soon to be no longer Imperial, there had, amongst others, been 'HM's' farewell for Azim. Between them 'HM' and Azim had divided the assets of the Government of India. Zeenat, Azim's wife, more glamorous than ever, had invited everybody to come and stay with them in Karachi. The ICS was withstanding the strain. At Iskander Mirza's farewell in a private suite of the Cecil Hotel in Old Delhi there had, by contrast, been a moment which augured ill for Indo-Pakistan relations. His last toast when we were leaving was a resounding 'Delhi Chalo!' (on to Delhi) as he smashed his champagne glass. Cycling back to New Delhi Maurice pointed out that Iskander was ex-Army and Political Department, not ICS.

Two days after independence when the Radcliffe Award was published, it created havoc. Sikh and Hindu refugees were streaming in. I was busy packing. Maurice, whose services had been terminated, had plenty of opportunity to listen to the foreign correspondents who shuttled between Delhi and Lahore. Theirs were horrendous tales. According to the BBC a hundred thousand people had been murdered in the Punjab. One press friend said that a woman was stabbed to death as she rushed into his arms; another watched, helpless, while six women were decapitated by a demented Sikh in Amritsar's railway station. The Sikhs were on the rampage in the Punjab. And slowly, as Sikh and Hindu refugees, fleeing retaliatory riots, poured in, Delhi's Sikhs began to organise reprisals.

I shall never forget the afternoon a young Sikh we knew stormed in for a friendly chat. Sikhs, according to their faith, had to wear a kirpan - a dagger - at all times. His kirpan had grown to menacing length. What did I think of his new slogan? 'Khun Khun se lagega!' (blood will call for blood).

'Don't you see, we *must* avenge our honour!' His cronies

were busy marking Muslim houses in Old Delhi 'like in the Bible with the Angel of Death, but in reverse.' Having failed to convince him that the place to avenge Sikh honour was in Lahore and Rawalpindi, not in Delhi where the Muslims had not killed or raped anybody, I threw him out.

On the third of September I started to keep a diary. I recorded that the dove nesting on our terrace no longer sat on her eggs and that it was so hot it had not prevented five dovelets from hatching by themselves a few days later. On the third evening the small bazaar facing our hostel and Nehru's residence burnt. The policemen at Nehru's gate did not interfere. A woman in burkha was sprayed with kerosene and set alight. They looked the other way.

Delhi came to a virtual standstill as shops were looted. The bigger stores closed, food ran out. Our hostel dining-room closed. I had a week's supply of Ostermilk. John would not starve.

On the 7th of September, according to my diary, Nehru fought a looting mob and took into his house some twenty Muslim women. Every evening he went to the same place in Delhi to appeal to the people to behave. Nobody took any notice. The Belgian Chargé d'Affaires came to dinner. We had nothing to offer him, not even cigarettes. He gave me half his last packet. On his way to us from Connaught Circus - perhaps two miles - he had counted seven corpses.

On the 8th of September, while I was trying to volunteer at the hospital, the Muslim servants in our hostel were evacuated to the Old Fort after a band of blood-stained Sikhs told Fonseca that they would burn his hostel if he harboured one single Muslim. Abdul, our bearer, was evacuated with the others. John's ayah said there was practically nothing left for the baba to eat. So I went over to Sushila Iengar to borrow some food. I found her in tears. Her house had been searched by the same blood-stained gang. However, the Iengars being South-Indian Brahmins had no Muslim servants. She accompanied me to her garden gate. A fresh corpse was leaning against it.

On the afternoon of the 8th Maurice began to help with the evacuation of Muslims to the Old Fort. Delhi airport having been attacked was closed. One heard shooting everywhere. Huge columns of smoke rose over Old Delhi. Hoping to find Farex and Ostermilk I cycled to Connaught Circus. Cycling through New Delhi was a weird experience. I felt quite safe amidst carnage. Nobody wanted to kill Europeans. The only risk was from a stray bullet. The road was littered with hideous sights. More disturbing than human corpses were the disembowelled horses abandoned to a slow death in the shafts of their tongas, with hovering vultures. Their only crime had been to belong to Muslim drivers.

There was this additional entry in my diary: '10 p.m. Mail, telephone, telegraph suspended. Staff afraid to leave their homes and families alone. Food scarce. Only 900 troops in Delhi. 1600 policemen out of 3000 have deserted. Sikhs tried to burn City Hospital because Muslim casualties treated there. Watched huge fire from roof top. Below in the road heard shouts of 'Allah O Akbar!' by Sikhs who kill those who answer. Doctor Sohoni* killed protecting Muslim children.'

My entry for September 9th reads as follows: 'Fires all night and day. Only six fire engines for Old and New Delhi. Gurkha and South-Indian battalions expected. No trains. Tried to get food for Abdul. Took whole morning to find one packet of Pretzels in Connaught Circus. Dropped in on Hélène who had watched the little shop opposite being looted and the shopkeeper being slashed. He ran for shelter to the backgarden of the *Daily Express* correspondent whose wife is hiding him. His hand was bleeding. She soaked it in her wash-basin and all the fingers fell off. Hélène had to make a tourniquet. She asked me to check the dressing. The

*a well-known New Delhi doctor and a Hindu.

bleeding had stopped. Lucky he was not killed. There are a few thousand Muslims in the Old Fort. Most have lost everything. Seen family killed. First chapati distribution since camp started. About 200 people fighting for chapatis. Left Abdul with Pretzels. Promised to come back. Maurice is trying to volunteer for night patrol.'

I spent most of the 10th trying to arrange a flight to Karachi for John and the ayah. He was booked, before the collapse, to fly to his grand-mother in London. Maurice wanted to show me Kashmir. A plane from Delhi made the connection for the Pan American flight from Karachi. Now all flights from Delhi to Karachi were requisitioned to transfer refugees, and the Willingdon Airport, Delhi's only airport, was closed. At the risk of incurring Maurice's anger I pulled strings, something which comes naturally to the French. Commander Galpin of BOAC was a friend. He promised to do his utmost. Even smuggle John on a refugee flight or divert the Bombay-Karachi flight to pick up our baby.

After seeing Commander Galpin I tried to volunteer for refugee relief work, but like Maurice, I found nobody to volunteer to. In the evening we walked across to the Iengars. Iengar was Nehru's Principal Private Secretary. He had just returned from an official tour of inspection of the Punjab with Nehru and Liaquat Ali, by now the Prime Minister of Pakistan. Iengar agreed with us that in Delhi the trouble was Sikh but he insisted that they had suffered great casualties in Lahore and the Punjab.

To occupy myself until time came for John to catch his plane, I made a detailed record of what Iengar said. His summary of the origin of the collapse of the Delhi government is as follows.

'First, on August 15th both sides were disorganised because a great number of the Muslim police, army and civil servants from India had opted for Pakistan. Only twelve ICS officers decided to stay in India, two of them in the North.

This left enormous gaps in the oveburdened machinery of Government. In Pakistan, on the other hand, the personnel from India had not had time to settle down and many people were new to their duties.

'Secondly, in India there were not enough troops because of the simultaneous withdrawal of all British troops and of bottlenecks in transferring three Sikh regiments from the NWFP where communications had broken down completely.

'Thirdly, communications by telephone and telegram had been cut off for six days as the result of Partition because Lahore, the key relay point, refused to transmit messages to and from India. Horrors went on on both sides with equal bestiality, unchecked. However, there was one difference. In India the army and the police were guilty of negative action, turning a blind eye, not protecting the minority. Because Sikhs and Hindus had suffered terribly in what was now Pakistan. In Pakistan, by contrast, the army and the police took positive action against minorities. Iengar quoted the case of Sheikhupura where a Baluch regiment blew up with mortars a factory in which some three hundred and fifty Sikhs had taken refuge, killing all three hundred and fifty. While this went on, the police, having declared a curfew, set fire to all Hindu and Sikh houses with the help of local Muslims and then proceeded to shoot, for breach of curfew, people running out of their houses. Iengar put the total casualties in Sheikhupura at some 6000 for that one day alone. What had upset him most was the visit to that factory.'

His story of what happened in Sheikhupura was confirmed to us later by three pressmen who had accompanied the Prime Ministers on their fact-finding tour.

John flew off on the 11th. Until the last minute it had been touch and go.

The British High Commission put at our disposal a jeep escorted by armed guards. The road was dotted with dead buffaloes. Tension at the airport was at fever pitch. A company of a Muslim regiment and a Hindu police detachment, both armed to the teeth, sten-guns at the ready, were patrolling the grounds, searching incoming and outgoing refugees for arms. Both units were from the Punjab. Battle could be triggered off at the slightest provocation. The airport was packed with refugees, mostly women and children, squatting on the ground without luggage. Some women were in the last stage of pregnancy, others carried newborn infants, all were terrified. Commander Galpin had diverted a plane from Bombay, it arrived three hours late, landed only long enough to pick up John and the ayah. As its door closed a belated downpour managed, in a matter of seconds, to transform the runway into a pond. We had to take our shoes off and wade through ankle-deep water. The women and children waiting to be evacuated were squatting in a hip-bath.

We were lucky to get a lift back in the car of Dewan Chamanlal, a prominent Congressman, who told us that at the latest meeting of the Cabinet Emergency Committee, the figures for casualties in Old and New Delhi had been put at between four and five thousand dead of which only three hundred were not Muslims. He, too, had toured the Punjab with Nehru and Liaquat Ali and said that the Deputy Commissioner Sheikhupura, an Anglo-Indian, had answered when asked by Nehru why he had not tried to prevent the massacre:

'Sir, I have opted for Pakistan so I felt I could not interfere.' While the killings went on he had had lunch in his bungalow and stayed there until it was all over.

By the time we got home the rain had stopped. Maurice cycled off to the Secretariat once more to volunteer. After tidying John's corner I brought my diary up to date.

There is a lacuna in the diary which no amount of trying to remember has filled. We had been cycling in Delhi quite freely without being stopped. Yet, according to my diary, there was a twenty-four hour curfew and the army was enforcing it ruthlessly. Had we been issued passes? Was the curfew in force only in Old Delhi? All I know is that the diary goes on to state that when Maurice did not return by midnight I became frantically worried. The day before Alan Campbell-Johnson, travelling in Mountbatten's car was shot at because the driver failed to slow down. The driver was killed, a passenger sitting next to Alan was injured. Alan had to climb to the front to get the wheel. The car, being Mountbatten's own, sported a large crown instead of a number plate. They also shot at a fire-engine killing one of the crew. By the time Maurice got back I was sobbing. His services had at last been accepted. He had been made Additional District Magistrate Delhi and put in charge of the transport department of the Joint Emergency Committee which was run by our friend 'HM'. It was an ad-hoc committee reporting to Nehru and Mountbatten. Its headquarters were in the Old Delhi Town Hall and its function was to keep the city going in the face of the riots.

The next day, the 12th, we both cycled to Old Delhi, . . . without passes? Maurice was trying to requisition lorries and trucks to cart away corpses. Corpses a week old were poisoning the air. It was most urgent to dispose of them to avoid epidemics. Cholera was already spreading in the Punjab. I was given an open truck and told to go into the old city to look for Muslims trapped in their homes and to take them to the Old Fort which by now had more than 25,000 refugees. To quote from my diary it had,

'only two water taps. Dead animals and dead people are lying on the streets. The stench is dreadful. Vultures are lazily picking. I found a young man with seventeen stab wounds and still alive. Maurice's collection of corpses is a long, tedious and dangerous job. He searches the entire city, house by house and risks being shot from a roof or a window, especially since the drivers are Sikh. In a deserted house he found an old woman alive; hands, breasts cut off.' After twelve hours without food we cycled back and went to bed.

On the 13th I went to Mr Roux, the French Minister, and asked him to lend me his car so that I could do a round of the homes of our friends to collect food for Abdul and his pals in the Old Fort. Being a diplomatic car it had to have an army escort. The armed guard was a Sikh, the driver a Hindu. For what happened at the Old Fort, back to my diary:

'We were surrounded by some fifty men yelling they would kill the guard if I did not remove him at once. I tried to point out we were bringing food. All they did was yell: "We are Muslims." A Baluch Army Captain in uniform was standing by, looking the other way. I told him to clear the crowd and protect the diplomatic car. The men were going to attack the car and remove the Sikh who was shaking like a leaf. The Captain answered:

"Madam, I am sorry but we are all Muslims and he is a Sikh." I got out of the car, stood between it and the men while the driver backed out as fast as he could. I had to carry the food into the camp alone. The driver was too scared to help and Abdul was too scared to come out. He said that before John left he had tried to say goodbye. He and another bearer had walked out of the Fort. They did not get very far. His companion was killed, stabbed from behind.'

At the hostel I found Sardar Panikkar. It was quite a shock. He had shaved the Lenin goatee of which he was so proud.

'I had to for safety. They might have mistaken me for a Muslim.' On his way to the UNO he had come to take his leave.

On the 14th of September we worked from the Town Hall non-stop from 8 am to 7 pm. Maurice was organising transport, not only to recover corpses but to move food supplies into Delhi. 'HM', who had given me that truck, insisted on an armed guard going with me. I did not like this, but as my driver was a Sikh I had to agree. To avoid being shot at from roof-tops I stood on the front seat next to the driver, holding on to the windscreen, in full view. Visibly a memsahib, in my bright red dress with green cherries. Loud speaker in hand I kept explaining I was a friend come to evacuate people trapped in their houses. The armed guard stood behind me, his rifle at a perilous angle towards my neck. I managed to persuade him to point it at the truck's floor. We evacuated a cholera case, a woman in labour, a few families and took food supplies to the Old Fort. I set up an information centre with boy-scouts. By late afternoon it was decided that Maurice would be in charge of a new refugee camp at Humayun's Tomb and that I would be his deputy.

Maurice, who had volunteered to lead a police patrol that night, sent me home saying he would drop in later to pick up a thermos flask filled with hot coffee and a cardigan. It must have been seven o'clock by the time I got home. I was preparing the thermos when a strange feeling came over me. Maurice would be killed that night. Certitude choked me. I had to sit down and think. Should I ask my husband not to go? But if he did not go, he would lose my respect - and my love. Could our marriage survive? I thought not. If he went just the same, my fear was bound to handicap him and might be the cause of his death. I must have sat for the best part of half an hour clutching that thermos flask, debating what to do. I would say nothing, kiss him goodbye and wish him luck.

Time was passing and I was still waiting for Maurice. By ten o'clock I could stand it no longer. He was going to be killed and I had not even kissed him goodbye. Unable to stay on my own I barged into the flat of the Daveys. Freda, the wife of my guardian angel, took one look at me and forced a peg of whisky down my throat. Only then was I able to speak. We sat, waiting, small talk abandoned. At half past eleven 'HM' dropped in on his way home to say he would send his car back for Maurice and the bike. They had been planning refugee evacuation and he had kept Maurice at the Town Hall to put the finishing touches to the plan.

Our friend, S N Misra went on that patrol instead of Maurice. He was murdered by his own policemen for trying to stop them from looting. The only Indian Civil Servant killed in the Partition riots. He left three widows and two small children.

Humayun's Tomb, the most prestigious of Delhi's Moghul Tombs, was well suited to become a refugee camp. The mausoleum stood in the centre of a vast walled garden. Archways and recesses provided natural shelters. When Maurice first sent me to investigate, on the afternoon of the 14th, he did not know it already housed refugees. A small group of Pathans, maybe 150 in all, hiding in fear for their lives. Pathans are both hated and feared in India because they are the only moneylenders who recover at the tip of their 'danda', a long stick with a heavy metal end. They had with them a dozen mules, some bed-rolls and odd belongings. The mules had eaten shrubs and grass, but the men had not eaten for a week. The leader, a turbanned Moses, welcomed me. Now that the tomb had become an official refugee camp they had to hide no longer. I explained that the guards at the entrance would protect them. With his help I drew up a list of necessities. Fire-wood, gram flour, salt, vegetables, and if possible some meat.

The old man was capable and responsible. He was obeyed. For the next couple of days he was my agent, distributing rations. But, as more and more refugees poured into the camp, his leadership collapsed. This happened on the third day, by which time there were some 20,000 refugees to look after. They would have obeyed him, but he could no longer assume responsibility. I was left alone in charge. Maurice was concentrating on bringing food to Delhi by truck and on transport in general. He only had a couple of hundred requisitioned trucks and lorries with which to provision Delhi, no mean task with no trains running. He sent me a young student from the All Indian Administrative Service College, Satarawala, a Parsee enthusiastic and able. He subsequently became Governor of the Punjab.

I left the routine of the camp administration to him to concentrate on liaison and supplies. I was much less likely to get shot than anybody else. In my red dress, standing in the front of the truck, holding on to the windscreen, everybody could see, from afar, that I was a Memsahib. I kept shuttling between the camp and old Delhi, bringing supplies and people who had been trapped in their homes.

On the 17th we received a cable, saying John had arrived in London.

Back to my diary for the 17th:

'All the monsoon in the world pelted down. The camp is flooded. People's belongings float in a vast lake. Over 17,000 refugees at last evening's count. Some have not eaten for four or five days. So much time wasted getting orders carried out, chasing coolies, getting through on the phone. One can go mad! I went to collect fuel from the Government depot. It is in a danger area and I felt scared. When I got there the coolies refused to load because it was getting dark and they were frightened. I managed to coax the driver and the guard to help me load. This did not shame the coolies into helping.

'The Chief Commissioner Delhi, one of the twelve ICS Muslims who opted for India, is as useful as an orchid in a famine! He came to see the camp. When I suggested that he made a broadcast on the loudspeaker system because the refugees were feeling miserable and scared he said:

'"I don't see why they are scared and miserable. I am pefectly happy."

'"So I see. Shame on you, a fellow Muslim and the Chief Commissioner!"

'The stabbing goes on. Maurice was walking in a crowded street when a man fell dead in front of him, a knife in his back. Maurice did not see the stabbing or notice anyone running away. My Sikh driver was murdered in his truck, inside the entrance to the Town Hall. When I got back I found him slumped on his wheel, a knife in the neck. There are fires here and there. Nothing is as grotesque as a water buffalo long dead. It looks like an anti-aircraft sausage with tiny legs sticking out. A lot of dead cattle are scattered on the roads. The vultures are so overfed that they are too lazy to fly. We ran one over today. Satarawala tells me that he can tell the difference between the smell of a dead horse, a dead man and a dead buffalo. I can't.

'September 21st. One of our Sikh drivers was shot by a soldier from a Baluch regiment at the Old Delhi Railway Station. Last night a lorry-load of Muslim villagers was driven into an ambush by an army driver. Thirty people were butchered and twenty five injured. So far Maurice's transport has collected 2700 corpses from Old Delhi and there are more. Some of the corpses are baby corpses, their heads dashed against the kerb or drowned in buckets like puppies. On the 19th I got James Walmsley extracted from the Ministry of Supply and made camp Commandant.'

By the time James came there were some 45,000 refugees in my camp, more than Satarawala and I could manage. James, a fellow ICS officer a couple of years senior to Maurice, had volunteered to stay on for a while. For a reason I have forgotten, 'HM' said James had to get his Minister to agree to release him before he could volunteer for the job. It was such a taxing job in such appalling conditions that he could not be posted automatically. Kotah House, James' hostel, was not far from ours. I went to ask him to help out. He was in his bath and the door was ajar. He did not jump at my proposition. I said I would not leave until he promised to volunteer. His clothes and his bath-towel were near me in the bedroom. As soon as James joined us I got Abdul out of the Old Fort to serve as his camp bearer. Conditions in the Old Fort were dreadful, much worse than ours. The camp Commandant had no authority, he had been besieged by the inmates, and Abdul said had been beaten up.

'2pm September 21st. This is my first lunch since I began to work and I want to use the little spare time on my diary.

James is first class, so is Satarawala. We make a good team. James stays in the camp, Satarawala does sanitation, I do requirements. We also have the invaluable help of a few soldiers from the Beds and Herts Regiment who have volunteered for picket and traffic duty. The Health Department of Delhi Province is useless. They have failed so far to provide any of the medical stores required. I must do the Sikhs justice: some of them behave admirably. Sir Datar Singh's son is a keen volunteer despite the fact that he has lost property worth more than 4 million pounds in the Punjab and little Rajendra Singh who works for Maurice in refugee transport, has just learnt that his mother, father and all his in-laws were murdered but he still carries on and refuses to take time off to comfort his wife. On the other hand, the volunteer in charge of food distribution in our camp, a Christian, is quitting because thirty members of his family have been killed in Lahore. He got the news yesterday. We will have to find a replacement. But where?

'This morning we had a lion and a tiger in the camp as well as their circus owner who made a great fuss when I had them shot. I also got the army to explode a water buffalo whose bloated carcass was threatening to contaminate the water supply: a line of taps near the entrance. One can no longer count on vultures to do the job.'

The Delhi Municipality having refused to provide containers for garbage, Satarawala and I filled my truck with the oil drums used as dustbins along New Delhi's avenues.

Spotting an old man asleep in his wheelbarrow I requisitioned it. KB Lall told me, years later, that tattered scraps of paper bearing my signature kept cropping up. As I had no official status, he had to redeem them from petty cash. 'My dear Taya, you were a real menace, kept haunting me: spades, wheelbarrows, especially buckets . . . You were insatiable!'

The 23rd of September was my birthday. That day the

monsoon fell with a vengeance.

'The camp has become a lake with cascades and streams. We wade in water up to our calves. The poor people! No food distribution today because of the rain. Our camp, we are told, is the best in India and Pakistan. I shudder to think of the others. The credit for our camp goes to James and the fact that it was under control from the start. But one has to be tough. Yesterday a crowd was looting tents. I stood on one side of the depot, kicking, shouting, while James, on the other side, was hitting with his shooting stick and cursing. We are not allowed to use British troops to keep law and order. Discipline has to be preserved at all costs. What can two men and one woman do against a large and desperate crowd? We have a few Gurkhas. When the Subedar Major refused to tell his men to stop the looting I slapped him across the face, in front of his men. He did not hit me back and his men stopped the looting. James said I was lucky to be alive.

'More trouble is brewing. A Muslim refugee train arrived in Pakistan with 166 killed. The next refugee train to India had one thousand dead aboard. My friend Fori is now helping full-time in the Town Hall, issuing requisition slips and assisting KB Lall who deals with supplies at the centre of things. She, and Lady Smith, the wife of Lt General Sir Arthur Smith, are admirable. Lady Smith is running our voluntary hospital with the help of Bishop Picket of the US Christian Mission and Dr Zakir Hussein of the Muslim College.*

'We had a visit from Rajen Nehru - the wife of another cousin of the Prime Minister. She came in a Red Cross van, spick and span, with an armed escort, to inspect our camp. When I suggested she get out to see for herself she said, quite calmly, that she knew every inch of the camp. More than James and I do. James nearly exploded. I said I fully

*Dr Zakir Hussein a noted educationalist was to become President of India.

understood her reluctance to muddy her sari. White, with a black and gold border, it was impeccably starched.'

There are times when one has to be ruthless. Because I was not ruthless enough we had cholera, some of which could have been avoided. From the very beginning I had been asking the Health Department for inoculations but they had paid no attention. A couple of days earlier a child had died of cholera. It was the first. When Lady Smith, in whose hospital-tent half a dozen infants were born daily, said she thought there was a child sick with cholera I rushed to get hold of the boy who was roughly the same age as our son. I carried him away, followed by the mother and told a young British private to take him to hospital with a note asking them to test for cholera and report at once. The mother begged me to let her come. Instinct told me to say no but, putting myself in her place, I said she could and saw mother and child into my truck with the private, fool that I was. The conscript left them for a minute, long enough for them to vanish. We looked everywhere. There were 67,000 refugees in the camp. I had lost my chance to prove it was not gastro-enteritis.

Two days later some sixty people died of cholera. The Health Department was, as I wrote in my diary: 'acting like ostriches, still calling it gastro-enteritis. Still no serum. This gives me the opportunity to report daily twenty or more cases of "mild stomach ache followed by death within six hours." I finally blew up and told Colonel Khan, the Head of the Health Department, what I thought of him. He came to the camp the next day with enough serum to inoculate 320 people, no needles or syringe. I had organised a squad of volunteer students, a couple of volunteer doctors and 8 medical students from the Lady Hardinge Hospital. I gave that *ass* hell. He came back with 4000 doses, one syringe and two needles! He is not alone in being stupidly incompetent. The President of the New Delhi Municipality, an engineer, objected to my digging latrines in the camp on the ground this would ruin beautiful lawns! Give an Englishman a piece of turf and he loses all sense of proportion.'

I was getting ready to leave the camp when the father of one of my volunteers rang to ask why his son had not returned. I had, off my own bat, gone to Dr Zakir Hussein for volunteers; being Muslim, they were safe inside the camp and every evening, after a roll call by their elected leader, they were bussed back under armed escort. Alerted, 'HM' sent a senior Indian Civil Servant to investigate. 'This is very serious. If anything has happened to the boy . . .'

Appeals on the loudspeaker system, cross examination of the guards, searches . . . all drew blanks. With a grim magisterial thoroughness, he began to sift the lack of evidence. No two witnesses told the same story. Had there been a roll call? The bus driver was positive there had been one but the student leader apologised for having skipped it as it was getting late and it looked as if everybody was there. Nobody had actually seen the boy board the bus. What was he doing before it was time to leave? He had, someone said, helped to dig a grave at the far end of the camp, near the gate leading to the railway siding. That was about a quarter of an hour before assembly time. Had he gone to help somebody? We rang up the volunteers who had telephones. They merely added contradiction to our confusion. Students were supposed to be picked up and dropped *inside* the university compound. It was not until close to midnight that the stupid boy remembered that, in the middle of major riots, his parents might worry because he had not come back. He had jumped off the bus as it passed a friend's house. I could have killed him!

We finally got a bulldozer to dig latrines. As soon as they were dug, James, Satarawala and I tried to enforce their use. Anybody caught defecating elsewhere was placed in a barbed wire enclosure and kept there for hours.

Later as the cholera epidemic spread we used the bulldozer to dig a pit, in which in disregard of Muslim funeral rites, we dumped the bodies, covering them with lime, instead of wrapping them in shrouds of virgin cloth.

Every day, at about six in the evening I went to the Town Hall where the officials of the Emergency Committee met under the Chairmanship of 'HM' to review the day's happenings and to plan for the morrow. Beside 'HM' who, as Cabinet Secretary reported to Mountbatten and Nehru, there were a couple of officials, three Muslim elders, Maurice, Brigadier Proud who looked after Army Supplies, and myself. Being the only non-official, non-English and non-Indian at the meeting, I alone could speak out freely to those who had not provided what had been asked of them. I suspect that 'HM' used me as his battering ram. Brigadier Proud used to call me 'tigress' and 'Oliver Twist'. I was always asking for more. More food. More volunteers. *More syringes*. When the Muslim elders' complaints poured oil on the fire and I could see, from the throbbing of an artery on 'H M's' forehead, that he had to exercise tremendous self-restraint, I would whisk out of my pocket a packet of fresh cardamom-pods and offer it round. Chewing cardamom has an astonishingly soothing effect.

'Taya's peace pipe,' said 'HM'.

Things were gradually improving. There were fewer stabbings and shootings. Getting about became safer. To make clear they were outside the fight, Indian Christians wore huge red crosses tacked to the front and the back of their shirts, modern version of the crusading knights. I even managed to persuade 'HM' to let me dispense with my armed escort. I had become such a familiar sight in Old Delhi, in my bright red dress, that I was not at risk and I managed to get, from our camp, a Muslim driver.

'September 25th. There are some 95,000 people in the camp which is still a lake. James has a cold. I have lost my voice. Children die of pneumonia and we have a full-blown cholera epidemic with 93 deaths in 3 days. Satarawala and I spend hours confiscating and burning food sold in illicit shops. That food is covered with flies; the water used for cooking it comes from the mud pools formed by the monsoon. People defecate and vomit in the water in which women wash their hair and their cooking pots.

'Since yesterday I feel a bit like a murderer. We got orders to evacuate people to Pakistan, that is the ones who want to emigrate. The Pakistan High Commissioner issued an unauthorised note telling them not to go as the way is not safe. I rang 'HM' from James' tented office. He told me it would be quite safe as he was sending 65 armed Gurkhas to protect the train. I asked the Pakistan official who had set up a makeshift office near James' tent to broadcast that a company of Gurkhas would escort the train. Instead he warned them not to go. In full view of thousands, I threw him out. The train with its armed escort duly arrived at the back of the camp. On a loudspeaker I personally guaranteed a safe journey to those who wanted to leave. Seven thousand left. Crammed inside and on top. The train was attacked in Patiala by the Maharajah's Sikh troops. When it arrived in Lahore it carried five hundred people who had been miraculously spared, three thousand five hundred injured and three thousand dead. The armed escort, true to Gurkha tradition, had been killed to a man, Hindus though they were. Evacuee trains have been stopped and cholera is spreading.'

It took me years to get over my sense of responsibility.

On the evening of the 26th I went to say goodbye to Hélène. Her usual smart self, for the past two weeks she had led a more or less normal, if restricted, life, lamenting the disappearance of her servants and the food shortage. To make up for such inconvenience, she had been playing bridge, thought of what she would be wearing next and designed clothes. Did I think that her verandah tailor, a Muslim, would come back? He was such a good tailor? And if he did not return, could I recommend a Sikh? She showed me turbans of tie-dyed muslin from Rajasthan, ideal for making into evening gowns. The next day we left.

We came back fifteen months later, Maurice for Unilever, I as a journalist.

WHO'S WHO

ABDUL	My bearer, (Factotum)
ABELL	Sir George, Private Secretary to the Viceroy.
ACKROYD	Prof, Leading nutrition expert, Head of Research at Coonoor.
ALEXANDER	A.V. UK Defence Minister
ALI	Asaf, Senior Muslim politician, Member Congress Working Committee.
ALINGTON	Peggy, Wife of senior administrator in Baluchistan.
ATIYAH	Beautiful wife of Muslim nobleman, she later worked for the BBC and became an author under the name of Hussein. Mother of Waris Hussein the TV Producer.
BAIG	Rashid, Muslim Sheriff of Bombay, later Indian Ambassador to Iran and Philippines.
BAIG	Tara, Wife of Rashid. Later became major figure in women's movements and in work for children.
BAPU	Affectionate name for Mahatma Gandhi
BHIL	Major aboriginal tribe of Western India.
BIJU	pet name, *see* B.K.Nehru
BOTTOMLEY	Arthur, British Parliamentary Under-Secretary of State for the Dominions.
BOWMAN	Johnny, Senior Bombay Official.
BRUNNER	Elizabeth, Painter.
CAMPBELL-JOHNSTON	Alan, Friend of Maurice's on Mountbatten's personal staff.
CHAMANLAL	Dewan, Senior Congressman from the Punjab.
CHOWDHURY	Mahomed Ali, Senior Muslim Official Ministry of Finance, later Prime Minister of

	Pakistan.
CLARENCE-SMITH	Jack, Senior Bombay Official, later Attorney General of Eritrea.
CLARENCE-SMITH	Mijeanne, Jack's French wife.
COOCH-BIHAR	Ayesha, Princess who became Maharanee of Jaipur and later an MP who was jailed during Indira Gandhi's Emergency.
CRIPPS	Sir Stafford, UK Minister for Economic Affairs
DALAL	Sir Ardeshir, Leading Parsee industrialist. Member of the Viceroy's Executive Council.
DALAL	Bobby, Friend of my husband and who later became the senior legal official of the Bombay Government.
DAMRY	Purviz, Friend of my husband and who later became Secretary of the World Bank.
DAMRY	Zarine, Purviz's wife and like her husband a skilled tiger hunter.
DAYAL	Harish, Offical of the Political Department later Indian Ambassador to Nepal. Husband of my friend Leela Row.
DESAI	Morarji, Chief Minister of Bombay, later Prime Minister of India.
DIAS	Tony, Friend of Maurice's, Bombay Official who became Governor of West Bengal.
DIAS	Joan, Tony's wife and my friend.
DIWAN	Prime Minister of a Princely State
DOON	Public School based on Eton.
FORI	Austrian wife of B K (Biju) Nehru and my friend.
FELL	Marjorie. Wife of Official in the Political Department.
GANDHI	Feroz, Parsee son-in-law of India's Prime Minister, later MP.
GANESH	Elephant-headed Hindu God of luck, son of

	Shiva and Parvati.
GOPAL	Ram, Indian dancer.
GWYER	Sir Maurice, Chancellor Delhi University and Chief Justice of the Federal Court of India.
HABIBULLAH	Sony, Taluqdar (nobleman) of Oudh. In Jinnah's inner circle, race-horse owner. Husband of Atiyah Hussein, father of Waris Hussein.
HUSSEIN	Sayed, Muslim protégé of Motilal Nehru who eloped with his benefactor's daughter.
HUSSEIN	Sheikh, Maurice's bearer (factotum).
HUSSEIN	Zakir, Muslim educationalist, later President of India.
HUTTEESINGH	Betty, Nehru's youngest sister, Bombay Socialite.
HUTTEESINGH	Raja, Gujerati millowner and Nehru's brother-in-law.
IENGAR	H.V.R. Nehru's Principal Private Secretary, later Governor of the Reserve Bank of India
IENGARS	Members of a Brahmin sub-caste of South India
IYERS	Members of another Brahmin sub-caste of South India.
ISHVARAN	One of Maurice's first bosses, later Indian Ambassador to Switzerland.
JACOB	British General who pacified Baluchistan.
JAINS	Followers of a religion of extreme non-violence.
JAT	Main peasant caste of the Punjab and the West U.P.
KAMALA	Nehru's wife and Indira Gandhi's mother.
KHADER	Abdul. My second Urdu teacher.
KHAN	Abdul Gafar, Muslim leader in the NWFP, follower of Gandhi
KHAN	Liaquat Ali, Finance Member Delhi, Pakistan's first Prime Minister.
KHAN	Saheb, brother of Abdul Gafar Khan,

	NWFP politician.
KHAN	Sir Sayyid Ahmad. Founder of the Muslim College, 1875, Spiritual father of Pakistan.
KITTY	Shiva Rao, Austrian theosophist wife of the correspondent of the *Manchester Guardian*.
KRAMRISCH	Stella, Professor of Indian Art, University of Calcutta and later Pennsylvania. Wife of my self-appointed riding instructor and great friend of mine.
LALL	K.B. Senior Official, later Secretary Commerce, Defence, Indian Ambasssador and Chairman of GATT.
LANGFORD	Jack, Senior Delhi official.
LANGFORD	Marie. Wife of Jack; sister of the Duchess of Sutherland.
LEDGARD	Colonel, Indian Medical Service.
LOW	Sir Francis, Editor of the British owned *Times of India.*
LUMLEY	Governor of Bombay; later Lord Scarborough
MACAULEY	Historian and poet; at one stage Member of the Viceroy's Executive Council.
MAHAVIRA	Ascetic Prince contemporary of the Buddha, founder of the Jain religious sect.
MASOOD	Senior Muslim Bombay Official who opted for Pakistan.
MATHAI	M.O. Adventurer who became Nehru's Eminence Grise.
MAYO COLL	Residential public school for princes.
MIRZA	Iskander, Senior Official of the Political Department, later Governor General of Pakistan.
MOORE	Mrs, famous hunter, wife of Chief Railway Engineer.
MOUNTBATTEN	Lord, Viceroy of India
NADKARNI	K. Bombay Official, later Chairman of the Port Trust.

	Lily, K's beautiful wife.
NAIDU	Dr, Son of Mrs Naidu; homoeopath and failed Communist.
NAIDU	Leelamani. Daughter of Mrs Naidu, Educationalist.
NAIDU	Padmaja. Daughter of Mrs Naidu. Later Governor of West Bengal.
NAIDU	Sarojini. Poetess, Congress leader, later Governor of the U.P.
NAIRS	Members of a caste from Kerala, a State in South India.
NAWAB	Muslim Prince or major nobleman.
NEHRU	B.K. (Biju). First cousin of India's Prime Minister, Senior Official before Independence, later Indian Ambassador in Washington and High Commissioner in London, then Governor of Kashmir.
NEHRU	Fori, Austrian wife of B.K.
NEHRU	Motilal. Father of India's first Prime Minister.
NEOGY	K.C. Congressman, later Minister in the Government of India.
NEMENYI	Hungarian Financial Adviser to the Finance Ministry first in Delhi later in Pakistan. My self-appointed riding instructor, husband of Prof. Kramrisch.
PANDIT	Sanskrit scholar; also courtesy title given to Kashmiri Brahmins.
PANDIT	Vijayalakshmi. Mrs. Nehru's sister, diplomat; later president of UN General Assembly.
PANDITA	Lady Sanskrit scholar.
PANIKKAR	Sadar, Prime Minister of Bikaner, Indian Ambassador to China and France. Historian.
PARSI(EE)	Believer in the Zoroastian religion.
PARVATI	Indian Goddess wife of Shiva.
PATEL	H.M. Senior Official Head of Cabinet Sec-

	retariat. Partition Secretary, later Secretary Defence, Principal Finance Secretary and Indian Finance and Home Minister.
PATEL	Sardar, Home Minister and later Deputy Prime Minister of India.
PETHWICK-LAWRENCE	UK Secretary of State of India
PREMY	Our son's Godmother; wife of Nitya Wagle, a friend and colleague of Maurice's. After independence in order to be able to travel Premy defeated the restrictions on foreign exchange by starting a very successful business of prêt-à-porter employing some 800 people.
QADIR	Manzur. Maurice's friend from Cambridge, Muslim lawyer, later Foreign Minister of Pakistan.
RAISMAN	Sir Jeremy, Finance Member, Government of India, later Deputy Chairman Lloyds Bank.
RAJPUT	Warrior Caste.
RAJIV	Nehru's grandson, later Prime Minister of India.
RAMA	Incarnation of the God Vishnu.
RAMADAN	Muslim month of fasting
RAMAYANA	Hindu Epic poem.
RANA	Fateh Singh. Bombay Official, son of a Muslim nobleman.
RAO	Shiva, Sir Rama Rau's brother, *Manchester Guardian* correspondent.
RAU	Lady Rama, Family Planning pioneer and Congress supporter. Premy's mother.
RAU	Sir Rama, Senior Indian Official. Chairman Bombay Port Trust, later Govenor of the Reserve Bank of India. It is interesting to note that brothers need not spell their surname the same way. This can be confusing.

RED SHIRTS	NWFP political party with affinities to Gandhi's Congress.
RIGVEDA	One of the sacred books of the Hindus.
RONALD	Dr, Austrian physician.
ROW	Leela, Indian tennis champion, dancer and Sanskrit scholar, wife of Harish Dayal and my friend.
ROY	Keith, Indian Official, Private Secretary to the Finance Member.
SANJAY	Nehru's second grandson.
SARABHAI	Mridula. Daughter of rich mill owner, Social Worker.
SARABHAI	Mrinalini, Dancer.
SATARAWALA	Young administrator, later Governor of the Punjab.
SEN GUPTA	Maurice's boss in the Ministry of Finance.
SHARIAR	Sultan, Politician. Later Foreign Minister of Indonesia.
SHARMA	Dr Biochemist, later Head of the Bangalore Institute of Science.
SHATTUCK	John, Senior Official Political Department.
SHIVA	Hindu God, husband of Parvati, father of Ganesh.
SHUNGLOO	Prime Minister of Jaisolmer.
SINGH	Ganga, Maharajah of Bikaner, a major Rajput State, Member of the War Cabinet during the First World war; ADC and friend of King George V.
SINGH	Hari. Our son's Godfather. Forestry Officer, later Inspector General of Forests, Government of India.
SINGH	Maharaj Nagendra (Nagu) Younger son of the Maharajah of Dungarpur. Maurice's colleague and friend; later President of the International Court of Justice at the Hague.
SINGH	Prem, my Urdu teacher.

SINGHANIA	Sir Padampat. Indian industrialist who became very rich during the war.
SONI	Sir Bagchand. Jain industrialist.
STIMSON	Bob, Correspondent of the BBC.
SYMINGTON	David, Secretary to the Governor of Bombay.
SYMONS	Ronnie, Senior Official Ministry of Finance, Government of India.
TALBOT	Philip, Correspondent of the *Chicago Tribune*, later US Ambassador to Greece at the time of the Colonels' Coup.
THAKURDAS	Sir Purshottamdas. Leading Bombay businessman trusted by all.
TUKER	Sir Francis, General Commanding Eastern Command. Commanded 4th Indian Division in the Desert during World War II.
TYMMS	Sir Frederick, Head of Civil Aviation, Government of India, later Director General of International Civil Aviation Organisation.
WADIA	Dina, Jinnah's daughter married to Neville Wadia.
WADIA	Neville, Jinnah's son-in-law; member of one of India's most respected industrial families.
WAGLE	Nitya, Bombay official married to Premy. Left Government service for industry, later President Bombay Chamber of Commerce.
WAGLE	Premy, Sir Rama Rau's daughter, our son's Godmother.
WALMSLEY	James, Senior Official, later Chairman of the Irish Chamber of Commerce.
WAVELL	Lord, Viceroy of India
WYATT	Woodrow, Secretary to the second Cripps Mission, now Lord Wyatt.
WYNT	Guy, Author and leader-writer on the *Manchester Guardian*.
YE	George, Foreign Minister of China under Chiang Kai Chek.

INDEX